Breed Standard for the Cavalier King Charles Spaniel

SIZE
Weight 5.4–8 kgs (12–18 lbs).

BODY
Short-coupled with good spring of rib. Level back.

COAT
Long, silky, free from curl. Slight wave permissible. Plenty of feathering. Totally free from trimming.

TAIL
Length in balance with body, well set on, carried happily but never much above the level of the back.

COLOURS
Black and Tan, Ruby, Blenheim, Tricolour. The Blenheim colour is unique for the Cavalier. It is described as rich chestnut markings well broken up, on a pearly white ground colour.

REAR LEGS
With moderate bone; well turned stifle without tendency to cow hocks or sickle hocks.

FEET
Compact, cushioned and well feathered.

Cavalier King Charles Spaniel

◇

by Juliette Cunliffe

Table of Contents

9

History of the Cavalier King Charles Spaniel

Examine the Cavalier's history as the author reveals its 15th-century beginnings in art and literature and become acquainted with the early European breeders and monarchs who brought attention to this delightful toy spaniel.

19

Characteristics of the Cavalier King Charles Spaniel

Discover what makes the Cavalier such a unique and adaptable dog: its practical size, glamorous but sensible appearance, charm and charisma all qualify the Cavalier as a happy and healthy pet for the right owner or family.

29

Breed Standard for the Cavalier King Charles Spaniel

Learn the requirements of a well-bred Cavalier by studying the description of the breed set forth in The Kennel Club standard. Both show dogs and pets must possess key characteristics as outlined in the breed standard.

34

Your Puppy Cavalier King Charles Spaniel

Be advised about choosing a reputable breeder and selecting a healthy, typical Cavalier puppy. Understand the responsibilities of ownership, including home preparation, acclimatization, the vet and prevention of common puppy problems.

PUBLISHED IN THE UNITED KINGDOM BY:

INTERPET
PUBLISHING

Vincent Lane, Dorking, Surrey RH4 3YX England

ISBN 1-902389-13-1

60

Everyday Care of Your Cavalier King Charles Spaniel

Enter into a sensible discussion of dietary and feeding considerations, exercise, grooming, travelling and identification of your dog. This chapter discusses Cavalier care for all stages of development.

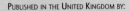

78

Housebreaking and Training Your Cavalier King Charles Spaniel *by Charlotte Schwartz*

Be informed about the importance of training your Cavalier, from the basics of housebreaking, and understanding the development of a young dog, to executing obedience commands (sit, stay, down, etc.).

Photo Credits

Photos by:
Carol Ann Johnson

Additional photos provided by:
Norvia Behling
Carolina Biological Supply
David Dalton
Doskocil
Isabelle Francais
James Hayden-Yoav

James R Hayden, RBP
Dwight R Kuhn
Dr Dennis Kunkel
Mikki Pet Products
Phototake
Jean Claude Revy
Dr Andrew Spielman
Karen Taylor
C James Webb

Illustrations by: Renée Low

101

Health Care of Your Cavalier King Charles Spaniel

Discover how to select a proper veterinary surgeon and care for your dog at all stages of life. Topics include vaccination scheduling, skin problems, dealing with external and internal parasites and the medical conditions common to the breed.

131

Your Senior Cavalier King Charles Spaniel

Recognise the signs of an ageing dog, both behavioural and medical; implement a senior-care programme with your veterinary surgeon and become comfortable with making the final decisions and arrangements for your senior Cavalier.

134

Showing Your Cavalier King Charles Spaniel

Experience the dog show world, including different types of shows and the making up of a champion. Go beyond the conformation ring to working trials, field and agility trials, etc.

Index: **156**

143

Understanding the Behaviour of Your Cavalier King Charles Spaniel

Learn to recognise and handle common behavioural problems in your Cavalier, including aggression with people and other dogs, chewing, barking, mounting, digging, jumping up, etc.

Cavalier King Charles Spaniel

The charming Cavalier King Charles Spaniel can trace its ancestors back to the small toy spaniels which are found in many paintings of the sixteenth, seventeenth and eighteenth centuries. Such dogs were favourites of royalty and nobles of the day and because of this many were depicted with their owners and with children, making for some delightful family groups. The first portrait in England that depicts the breed is one of Queen Mary I with her husband, Philip of Spain, accompanied by a pair of small spaniels lying at their feet. It was painted in 1554 by Antonio Moro. Well-respected artists such as Titian, Van Dyck, Stubbs, Gainsborough and Reynolds all showed similar small dogs with flat heads, high-set ears and a slightly pointed noses.

It was a little black and white toy spaniel that hid beneath the skirts of Mary Queen of Scots at her execution in 1587. Even after her death, it would not leave its dead mistress for it was recorded, 'Then one of the executioners, pulling off her garters, espied her little dogg which was crept under her clothes which could not be gotten forth but by force, yet afterwards would not depart from the dead corpse, but came and lay between her head and her shoulders…'

During Tudor times (1485–1603) these small spaniels were highly popular as ladies' pets and under the House of Stuart (1603–1714) they were actually given the name King Charles Spaniels. King Charles I was accompanied by a small spaniel when he was a fugitive at Carisbrook Castle. After he had

Opposite page: Posing for a portrait must be counted amongst the Cavalier King Charles Spaniel's natural abilities. These lovely dogs have sat for many famous painters (and photographers!).

Sir Edwin Landseer was the artist of choice for Queen Victoria and Prince Albert, for whom he painted a series of portraits depicting court life at Windsor. From 1845, this famous Landseer painting is entitled *Cavalier's Pets.*

9

been executed, his dog, Rogue, was paraded around the city by a Roundhead, though the fate of the little dog is not known. But it was really thanks to King Charles II that the breed took its name.

A great lover of these dogs, Charles II was almost always seen with some of his small canine friends at his heels. The famous diarist Samuel Pepys made many references to them, showing dismay that the King played all the while with his dogs rather than minding business affairs. The King even decreed that these spaniels were to be allowed in any public place, including the Houses of Parliament, somewhere in which dogs were not usually permitted.

James II was another king reputed to be fond of the breed, and there is record of him giving orders during a bad sea storm that the men were to 'save the dogs! ... and the Duke of

Monmouth!' One can only wonder if there was any significance in his mentioning the dogs before the Duke! Undoubtedly spaniels of this kind were much in favour in many of the European courts, but although the red and white variety bred at Blenheim Palace retained its popularity, the others seemed to go somewhat out of fashion. This was thanks largely to the accession to the throne of William and Mary, their favourites being Pugs.

The merry toy spaniels that had scampered about the palaces and had appeared on numerous state occasions were, it might be said, demoted by the House of Orange. The Pugs smugly took their place. Some believe that it was because of the newfound popularity of the Pug that some enthusiasts of King Charles Spaniels decided that a certain change in the breed's features would perhaps be an improvement.

During the early years of the nineteenth century, the small spaniel once again rose in the popularity stakes for the Duke of Marlborough used small spaniels as shooting companions. These were a little larger than the Cavaliers known today. In 1820 his dogs were described as 'very small or carpet spaniels.' They were red and white, with very long ears, short noses and black

DID YOU KNOW?
Some people believe that all spaniels originated in Spain and that they actually took their name from the word 'espagnol,' which means Spanish. It is also believed that the black Truffle Dog may lie behind black and tan coloured Cavaliers.

eyes. Still today, what is known as the lozenge spot on the head of some Cavalier King Charles Spaniels is highly prized, and there is a delightful story as to how this came about. The Duchess of Marlborough had one of these spaniels as a much-loved pet which kept her company whilst her husband was away at war. At anxious times she had the habit of pressing her thumb

Once known as Gredin, the black Cavalier of yesterday much resembles the variety we know as Black and Tan.

on her dog's head whilst awaiting news of her husband. When the bitch produced a litter of puppies the head of each was marked with her thumbprint.

Hitherto these spaniels had been brown and white, black and white or tricolour. In the past there were black spaniels but they were known as Gredin, although they were very much like today's black and tans, with tan eyebrows, muzzles, throats

and legs, known as 'fire-marks.' It was not until the reign of Queen Victoria that ruby-coloured spaniels appeared. In her youth, Queen Victoria owned a small spaniel called Dash, a tricolour. So fond was she of Dash that after her Coronation in 1838 she was said to have rushed home to give her dog its usual bath. Dash was a familiar little figure and appeared on many pieces of needlework sewn by Victorian women. The first known painting of a ruby is one in which the Duke and Duchess of Cumberland were pictured walking with such a dog. A gentleman by the name of Mr

The ever-popular red and white Cavalier, called the Blenheim, received its name from the Blenheim Palace where the dogs were bred.

DID YOU KNOW?
Although the true origin of today's Cavalier is not really known, the breed may originally have developed from a red and white spaniel of Malta or Italy, this having been crossed in the thirteenth century with a type of spaniel from the Far East.

11

The Ruby coloured Cavalier has been known since the late nineteenth century. It has never been as popular as the other three varieties.

The Pug was likely incorporated into Cavalier stock to bring about the shorter faced, flat-headed King Charles breed.

programmes in order to help bring about this significant change. In 1886 the Toy Spaniel Club was founded, but in 1902 the organisation changed its name to the King Charles Spaniel Club, even though initially The Kennel Club was opposed to this change of name. Once again royal interest worked in favour of the breed and Edward VII

Risum is reputed to have owned the first known ruby and this won second prize at the Alexandra Palace Show in 1875.

Undoubtedly in the early years both size and type varied within the breed, so it may be surmised that at that time breeding was carried out in something of a haphazard way. However, as the nineteenth century moved on in Britain, dog showing was starting to become a popular pastime and the breed saw a new fashion emerge. Soon enough the so-called 'old type' had begun to disappear: the longer nosed, flat-headed dogs having been replaced by a much shorter faced, dome-headed dog now known as the King Charles. It was believed that the Pug may have been used in breeding

intervened, subsequent to which the new name was approved.

The First World War had a disastrous effect on King Charles Spaniels, as indeed it did on so

DID YOU KNOW?
During the sixteenth century, ladies used small spaniels to keep themselves warm and cosy. They sat on ladies' laps and provided some measure of protection against draughts in cold houses and on journeys in carriages.

many breeds of dog. An American gentleman by the name of Roswell Eldridge had been to Britain to search for a pair of these dogs and dearly wanted to re-kindle interest in the breed.

In the Crufts show schedule for 1926, King Charles Spaniel enthusiasts were startled by an announcement that this same Mr Roswell Eldridge of New York was offering two prizes of £25 each for 'Blenheim spaniels of the old type as shown in Charles II's time: long face, no stop, flat skull not inclined to be domed, with spot in centre of skull.' This was a far cry from the King Charles being shown at that time. Interestingly the suggested models to comply with this stipulation were those shown in Landseer's painting, despite the fact that these did have a slight indentation between the eyes, known as a stop. Although this was shallow, the request for no stop was probably rather confusing for exhibitors, especially those who had already spent many years actually developing a more 'squashed-in' nose, with a more accentuated stop and a domed skull.

To begin with, there were few competitors for the special prizes on offer, but a handful of breeders decided to re-develop the Toy Spaniels according to Mr Eldridge's definition. Two years

A Tricoloured Cavalier, the variety preferred by Queen Victoria, is black and tan with a white ground colour.

later, in 1928, a special club was formed for this particular type, although there were then still very few of them. The selection of a name caused much heart-searching for breeders did not want to lose the name 'King Charles.' Eventually the name 'Cavalier King Charles Spaniel' was selected. A standard of points was drawn up for the breed, using Ann's Son, an early

DID YOU KNOW?

Amongst many well-known people who have owned Cavalier King Charles Spaniels in recent years are Her Royal Highness Princess Margaret, Nigel Lawson the politician and former President Ronald and First Lady Nancy Reagan of the U.S.

winner of Mr Eldridge's prize, as the dog on which the standard was based. In fact it is Ann's Son and five other dogs that really formed the foundation of the Cavalier King Charles Spaniel we know today.

However, things could not progress as quickly as may have been wished. There were still only few dogs in number and The Kennel Club was not prepared to grant the breed separate status, indeed not for the next seventeen years! Meanwhile these dogs were known as King Charles Spaniels (old type) and were shown in the same classes as the King Charles.

In 1945 The Kennel Club thought it right to grant separate classification to the Cavalier King Charles Spaniel and to grant the breed championship status. Sadly Mr Roswell Eldridge had died long before, in 1928, so he did not have the fulfilment of knowing that the dogs he so loved had gained official recognition. The first Championship Show for the breed was held at Stratford-upon-Avon on August 29th, 1946, when Best in Show was awarded to Mrs Eldred's Belinda of Saxham, a Blenheim. The first Cavalier to gain its

The Cavalier King Charles Spaniel was recognised as a separate breed by The Kennel Club in 1945. In no time at all it became the most popular Toy dog in Britain.

Championship title, this in 1948, was Daywell Roger, who had been awarded Best Dog at the first Championship Show. He was a successful sire with several champion offspring who were to have great influence on the breed in the years ahead.

The King Charles Spaniel, also known as the English Toy Spaniel, has fallen in popularity, whilst the Cavalier has topped the list of the country's most popular dogs.

The breed quickly gained popularity in Britain and amongst the Toy breeds was only surpassed in popularity by what were then described as the 'rave breeds,' Yorkshire Terrier, Pekingese and Smooth Coated Chihuahuas. In Britain between the years 1954 and 1964, the number of Kennel Club annual registrations for the breed had risen from 794 to 2,352, by which time registrations for the King Charles Spaniel amounted only to 170. By 1966 the Cavalier climbed into The Kennel Club's 'Top Twenty' list of breeds. This was undoubtedly in part because the breed was by then winning well at shows. In 1963 Amelia of Laguna had won Best Toy at Crufts and then Best Bitch of all breeds on the first day of the show, whilst in New Zealand a Cavalier by the name of Sugar Crisp of Ttiweh had won Best in Show all breeds at a Championship Show. There was no turning back now.

As the 1960s drew to their close, Britain's Cavalier King Charles Spaniel Club had over 400 members, comprising a keen and lively body of people, helped and encouraged by its officers and committee. Many Cavaliers have won high accolades at shows and in 1973 Alansmere Aquarius, owned by Messrs Hall and Evans, won what is perhaps the most famous award of all, Best in Show at Crufts.

In Europe the Cavalier King

Charles Spaniel is shown under the rules of the Fédération Cynologique Internationale (FCI) in Group 9 and in Section 7, which is for English Toy Spaniels, the other breed in this group being the King Charles. The Cavalier is also divided by colour into: a) Black and tan, b) Ruby, c) Blenheim and d) Tricolour. The number of

DID YOU KNOW?

A member of King Charles II's court complained about the general doggy disorder in the King's apartments. One of the main complaints it seems was that the King permitted the dogs to whelp in his own bedroom!

entries at European shows varies considerably according to the country and the prestige of the show, ease of accessibility and so on. The World Show moves from country to country and can attract approaching 100 Cavaliers, whereas at Crufts there may be as many as 400 or more.

In mainland Europe, Cavaliers had become fairly popular in Holland during the breed's relatively early days, and certain interest in the breed was also expressed in Germany and in Italy. In Sweden the Cavalier went from strength to strength with registrations rising rapidly

A young Ruby Cavalier with a promising show career ahead of it.

through the 1960s and 1970s, and now the breed has captivated the hearts of numerous dedicated breeders in many countries throughout the world.

In the U.S., the King Charles Spaniel is known as the English Toy Spaniel and is divided into separate classifications for solid and parti-colours. However, there were only five Cavaliers in the country when Lady Forwood sent one over as a gift in 1952. The first breed club was established in the U.S. in 1956. From the early 1960s the Cavalier was shown in the American Kennel Club's Miscellaneous classes but finally, on January 1st, 1996, it officially became the AKC's 140th recognised breed. In the U.S. the breed also competes regularly in obedience trials.

In Canada the breed gained recognition in 1957, and by 1964 a small number of Cavaliers were being shown. The following year,

Who could better the description, 'one of the nicest, best mannered dogs' to sum up the Cavalier?

1965, saw the breed's first Canadian Champion, Pargeter Flashback. Since then the breed has grown enormously in popularity, and in recent years has often found itself with the largest entry in the Toy Group at shows.

The breed did not arrive in Australia until 1960 where the Cavalier's early history centred primarily around dogs in Victoria, New South Wales and Western Australia. The Blenheim bitch, Soyland Begonia, imported in whelp from New Zealand, was to become the country's first champion. Numbers grew steadily from then on, especially during the 1970s, and in 1978

Lady Forward, Patron of the New South Wales Club, was invited to judge the tenth anniversary show, beginning a tradition of continued co-operation with Cavalier breed enthusiasts throughout the world.

When writing about the breed in 1970, authors Margaret Sheldon and Barbara Lockwood said that the Cavalier King Charles Spaniel was 'certainly one of the nicest, best mannered dogs on the Toy register. One almost expects him to sweep-off his finely plumed hat and give one a deep, courtly bow!'. As I would find it difficult to better this description, I shall close this chapter here in the hope you will agree.

17

CHARACTERISTICS OF THE
Cavalier King Charles Spaniel

There are many excellent reasons why one should select the Cavalier King Charles Spaniel as a pet, or even as a show dog. This is an affectionate, playful, intelligent, small dog that is only too willing to repay an owner's care and attention with complete devotion.

Although undoubtedly considered a lap dog because of its size, the Cavalier is an absolutely fearless, sporting little dog. He is gay, friendly and non-aggressive and makes an excellent and adaptable companion for many different homes and lifestyles.

PHYSICAL CHARACTERISTICS

This is undisputedly a small breed, but one that is neither too small nor too delicate. The largest of the breeds within the Toy Group, the Cavalier is considerably larger than the King Charles that weighs on average about 1.8 kgs (4 lbs) less. Cavaliers do vary quite considerably in size, but, according to The Kennel Club's breed standard, should weigh between 5.4 and 8 kgs (12–18 lbs).

The disparity in size between the different Cavaliers one comes across can easily confuse those not familiar with the breed. The bone is fairly heavy and so a small dog can weigh perhaps more than one could expect at first glance. On the other hand, a taller, more lightly boned Cavalier may actually weigh less than a smaller representative of the breed. However, this is a Toy breed and should in no way compare, for example, to a small Welsh Springer Spaniel.

It is within most people's capacity to pick up and carry the Cavalier when necessary, and at shows this breed is lifted onto a table for assessment by the judge. Because it such a charming breed it is often a good choice of dog to be shown by children. Indeed, it can be quite amusing to see a young girl lifting her patient charge high onto the judge's table for assessment, often her own little face barely peeping above the dog's back, and yet the Cavalier seems to take this all in its stride!

Because of the breed's practical size, the Cavalier is also assessed on the table for veterinary examination, and when in the waiting room can be held on one's lap, rather than being placed on the floor.

Opposite page: The Cavalier King Charles Spaniel is a pet who quickly adapts to the lifestyle of its keeper—whether a city life or a country one.

Whether you lead an active lifestyle or a more sedentary one, your Cavalier will happily accompany you. Discuss your lifestyle with your breeder before selecting your puppy.

Cavalier King Charles Spaniels are as handsome as they are personable and loving. Given the proper training and attention, the Cavalier can delight most any one!

A Cavalier King Charles Spaniel is also a highly suitable breed to carry in a dog crate, something which is especially useful when travelling by car for this safety measure prevents the chance of escape when doors are opened or in case of accident.

PERSONALITY

The Cavalier King Charles Spaniel can be equally at home with a large, boisterous family as it can with a single person, whatever that person's age. Having said that, children should always be instructed never to handle a dog too roughly, nor should they be permitted to tug at the coat. The breed can be happy living with energetic owners who are likely to take their dog out on long, exciting walks, but can also live a comfortable and happy life following a more sedentary existence. When living with a less active family, the dog must be afforded ample opportunity for exercise and activity to avoid obesity. This is a factor that must be considered when taking on any breed of dog.

The amenable Cavalier will generally adapt to whatever lifestyle is offered and will adapt readily to a regular short walk around the block, a longer walk with a free romp in the park, or merely a good energetic game with a ball in the garden. At other times of day the Cavalier will be quite content to join his owner watching the TV, curled up on the sofa or resting comfortably in a corner of the sitting room. The Cavalier is a breed that is often

described as 'a people dog,' one that appreciates, enjoys and indeed needs human company.

The Cavalier King Charles Spaniel generally gets on well with other dogs and household pets, rarely showing any particular jealousy or possessiveness over titbits or favourite toys. Of course, when introducing any dog to a new companion, caution must be exercised on the part of the owner, but in the case of Cavaliers such introduction is rarely overly stressful for any party concerned. Like many other breeds, Cavaliers seem to thoroughly enjoy the company of other dogs. Many owners like to keep a couple of Cavaliers as pets, as they make for happy companionship and are so easy to look after. Owning and caring for two requires little more work than just one. Although no dog owner should regularly leave dogs alone for long periods, a Cavalier will usually appreciate the company of a canine companion if his owner does have to be away from home for a few hours from time to time.

Except when hunting, the Cavalier is not really a very independent breed, but instead is one which prefers to rely on a pack leader and, of course, the pack leader is, or should be, the dog's owner.

This is not a breed of dog that should be left outside all day in a kennel situation. Instead it is a pet, a canine companion that prefers to be involved in human activity so should be allowed to live within the household as a family companion, however large or small the 'family'. In the mind of an adoring dog, one owner is quite sufficient as a 'family,' provided that person gives him every care and attention he needs and deserves.

We all know that there are exceptions to every rule, but this is not what might be described as a 'yappy' dog. Like most dogs the Cavalier will bark if there is a stranger about. Despite this, the Cavalier is not suitable as a guarding breed for its very nature is too soft to deter any intruder!

Although there are certainly Cavaliers that are obedience trained, many owners claim their dogs have absolutely no road sense, so it is always wise to walk your dog on a lead in any public place. Although the Cavalier does not have the long legs of breeds like the Whippet or Greyhound, it is surprising how quickly those little legs can move. One must

DID YOU KNOW?

Most smaller breeds of dog tend to live longer than very large, heavy ones. The Cavalier King Charles Spaniel can be expected to live on average for 11 to 12 years, sometimes longer.

Though rarely thought of as field dogs, the Cavaliers are, after all, spaniels. Given the proper training, they can perform well under many field and hunting conditions.

always be aware that the safety of one's dog is of paramount importance and that a dog on the loose in the wrong place can also cause danger to others and cause traffic accidents.

COLOURS AND COAT

Apart from the breed's attractiveness in ease of size, management and personality, it is the Cavalier's glorious array of striking colours that endears many people to this lovely breed. The range of colours now includes Blenheim, Ruby, Black and Tan and Tricolour, of which the Blenheims are the most numerous. These are generally the easiest to obtain for when a dog and bitch of this colour are mated

together they always produce Blenheims, no matter what other colours are involved in the genetic background. Certainly the Blenheims with their rich tan and white markings are incredibly striking, and those that possess a lozenge mark on the head are very highly prized. Markings should, if possible, be evenly distributed on the head, and markings that are not symmetrical are likely to be penalised in the show ring.

Ideally both Blenheims and Tricolours should have their markings well broken up. Tricolours are black and white with tan markings over the eyes, on cheeks, inside the ears and legs, as well as on the underside of the tail. Again, a judge will look for the placement of these markings in a show dog. It is not always realised that the prized lozenge mark can also be found in Tricolours.

Black and tan can be yet another striking colour combination. The black should be what is described as 'raven black' and the tan markings should ideally be found above the eyes, on cheeks, inside ears, on chest, legs and on the underside of the tail. These tan markings should be bright but any white found on the coat is undesirable. Technically, a Cavalier that is black and tan is described as a 'whole colour' and any white found in the coat would therefore be incorrect. There are not a great many black and tan Cavaliers to be found, so obtaining one of this colour may indeed be difficult, or could involve a long wait. However, sometimes black and tans that show just a little white in their coat are available as pets for they would be penalised heavily in the show ring.

Rubies are whole coloured in a rich red and, like black and tans, any white on the coat is undesirable. Having said that, sometimes ruby puppies are born with a small fleck of white on the head, but this will usually have disappeared by seven or eight months of age. Because, genetically, the ruby colouring is the most

difficult to breed true, this colour is not easily found.

Whatever the colour of one's Cavalier, the coat will require regular grooming if it is to be kept in all its glory. Nonetheless, compared with some other breeds, the amount of grooming required is not excessive. The Cavalier is quite small and does not have as much coat as a Maltese or Rough Collie, for example.

Whether one decides to have a dog or a bitch as one's pet is very much a matter of personal preference and factors such as a bitch's coming into season will undoubt-edly have some bearing on the final decision. However, it may also be worth bearing in mind that males do tend to have a little more coat than females, which can make them rather more glamorous. Males may also need just a little more time spent in grooming than females. Conversely, a female Cavalier that has recently been in season will usually 'drop' coat. During this season, it is sensible management of the coat to keep one's pet in tip-top condition.

TAILS AND DEW CLAWS
Docking of tails is now a subject under some debate, especially by the veterinary profession. However, historically the docking of tails on Cavalier King Charles

The Cavalier requires daily brushing and combing to keep its soft and luxurious coat in good condition.

Spaniels has been optional but, if done, it should have been carried out within the first few days of life and more than one-third of the tail should not have been removed.

Dew claws are usually removed, but again this must be done at a very early age, usually on the third or fourth day. In Britain this procedure must be carried out by a veterinary surgeon. Cavaliers rarely have dew claws on the hind legs, but they should always be checked so that they are not left on unintentionally. The reason for removal of dew claws is not just an aesthetic consideration but avoids these claws, which are not functional in most breeds, from being torn when out running and exercising.

A CAVALIER'S I.Q.

By normal canine standards, the Cavalier King Charles Spaniel has a fairly high I.Q. and many of their senses, such as smell and hearing, are more highly developed than those of humans. But even though a Cavalier fits in so well with home life, they do not, as some would like to believe, have near-human mentality. They are easily able to assimilate the fears and joys of their owners, so it follows that a somewhat nervous person may convey that feeling to the dog, which may well end up with a rather similar personality.

Conversely, a highly boisterous or bubbly person is likely to end up with a Cavalier with a similar personality.

HEALTH CONSIDERATIONS

Many dogs, whatever their breed, suffer health problems at some time during their lives, but undoubtedly some breeds seem more prone to certain problems than others. If one knows what to look out for, owners can be prepared to seek urgent veterinary advice so that hopefully any problems that may occur can be caught in the nick of time. This will facilitate a greater chance of recovery if possible, or management of the disease if it is one which is incurable.

Most Cavaliers are healthy little dogs but care must be taken to ensure that they do not put on too much weight. Obesity, however slight, can put additional stress on the heart, and some Cavalier have a tendency to suffer from heart problems. Of course many Cavaliers live long and healthy lives, but one should be aware that the apparent onset of heart conditions in the breed is usually around eight years, sometimes a little earlier. Because of the breed's appealing eyes, many are fed table scraps without sufficient thought. However, it is much kinder to your dog in the long term to feed a healthy diet and keep treats

problems and are encouraged to have both parents eye tested prior to arranging a mating.

Not really a health problem, but something that can be perplexing and sometimes frightening for an owner is the breed's habit of snorting. This sounds rather like a choking cough but can easily be stopped by placing the hand over the dog's nose just for a few seconds. This causes the dog to open its mouth and clear the airway.

Because Cavaliers are fairly hardy dogs and can thoroughly enjoy a sporting life, they are also good water dogs. However, if a dog gets wet, especially in cold weather, it is essential to dry the coat so that the dog does not sit around for long periods feeling damp. This could lead to long-term joint problems, which might otherwise be avoided, not to mention possibly causing a chill!

only to sensible ones, certainly not chocolates and little pieces of cake, however tempting they may be!

Occasionally Cavalier King Charles Spaniels also suffer from hereditary cataracts (HD) and multi-focal retinal dysplasia (MRD); in Britain the breed is on Schedule 1 of the BVA/KC/ISDS scheme for these eye disorders. The breed is currently under investigation for multi-ocular defects which include any combination of nystagmus, microphthalmos, PPM, CHC and RD.

This all sounds rather alarming but good breeders have their stock screened for heart

DID YOU KNOW?

The Cavalier King Charles Spaniel has always been considered a natural breed and enthusiasts have tried hard to keep it that way. This has helped the Cavalier to remain an unexaggerated breed of dog, not one that requires great artistry in coat presentation for the show ring, although it must, of course, always be well groomed.

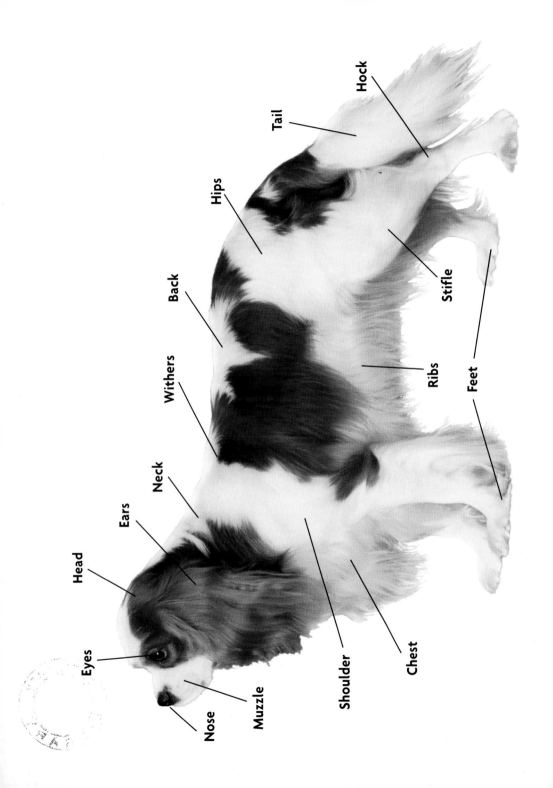

Hock

Tail

Hips

Stifle

Back

Ribs

Withers

Feet

Neck

Ears

Head

Shoulder

Eyes

Chest

Nose

Muzzle

BREED STANDARD FOR THE
Cavalier King Charles Spaniel

The breed standard for the Cavalier King Charles Spaniel is considered a 'blue-print' for the breed. Effectively the various points of the dog are written down in such a way that a visual picture can be conjured up in one's mind. However, this is more easily said than done. Not only do standards vary slightly from country to country but people's interpretations of these breed standards vary also. It is this that makes judges select different dogs for top honours, for each person's idea of which dog most closely fits the breed standard varies, albeit just slightly. That is not to say that a good dog does not win regularly under different judges, whilst an inferior dog may rarely even be placed at shows, at least not amongst quality competition.

The breed standard given here is that authorised by The Kennel Club. You will notice that no height is given for the Cavalier in England, and yet in America the height is actually specified as 12–13 inches, which is about 30.5–33 cms. Also, in the U.S. the weight range starts at 13 lbs as opposed to 12 lbs in the U.K. It may seem hardly relevant to mention these things but they are important for a dog which is underweight in America but might be acceptable in Britain, where the breed is neither measured nor weighed in the ring.

THE KENNEL CLUB STANDARD FOR THE CAVALIER KING CHARLES SPANIEL
General Appearance: Active, graceful and well-balanced, with gentle expression.

Characteristics: Sporting, affectionate, absolutely fearless.

Temperament: Gay, friendly, non-aggressive; no tendency to nervousness.

Head and Skull: Skull almost flat between ears. Stop shallow. Length from base of stop to tip of nose about 3.8 cms (1.5 ins). Nostrils black and well developed without flesh marks, muzzle well tapered. Lips well developed but not pendulous. Face well filled below eyes. Any tendency to snipiness undesirable.

Eyes: Large, dark, round but not prominent; spaced well apart.

The skull should be almost flat between the ears.

Feet: Compact, cushioned and well feathered.

Tail: Length of tail in balance with body, well set on, carried happily but never much above the level of the back. Docking optional, no more than one-third to be removed.

Gait/Movement: Free-moving and elegant in action, plenty of drive from behind. Forelegs and hindlegs move parallel when viewed from in front and behind.

Coat: Long, silky, free from curl. Slight wave permissible. Plenty of feathering. Totally free from trimming.

Ears: Long, set high, with plenty of feather.

Mouth: Jaws strong, with a perfect, regular and complete scissor bite, i.e., upper teeth closely overlapping lower teeth and set square to the jaws.

Neck: Moderate length, slightly arched.

Forequarters: Chest moderate, shoulders well laid back; straight legs moderately boned.

Body: Short-coupled with good spring of rib. Level back.

Hindquarters: Legs with moderate bone; well turned stifle—no tendency to cowhocks or sickle-hocks.

Colour: Recognised colours are:
Black and Tan: Raven black with tan markings above the eyes, on cheeks, inside ears, on chest and legs and underside of tail. Tan should be bright. White marks undesirable.
Ruby: Whole coloured rich red. White markings undesirable.
Blenheim: Rich chestnut markings well broken up, on pearly white ground. Markings evenly divided on head, leaving room between ears for much valued lozenge mark or spot (a unique characteristic of the breed).
Tricolour: Black and white with well spaced, broken up, with tan markings over eyes, cheeks,

Cavaliers come in four colour varieties. The standard describes precisely what comprises each colour variety.

inside ears, inside legs, and on underside of tail.

Any other colour or combination of colours highly undesirable.

Size: Weight: 5.4–8 kgs (12–18 lbs). A small, well balanced dog well within these weights desirable.

Faults: Any departure from the foregoing points should be considered a fault and the seriousness with which the fault should be regarded should be in exact proportion to its degree.

Note: Male animals should have two apparently normal testicles fully descended into the scrotum.

It would, of course, be possible to analyse the breed standard in great detail, but readers who are interested in showing their Cavalier should learn as much as possible from more established breeders and exhibitors, and should attend specialist breed seminars so that the finer points of the breed can be explained in depth. However, there are several points in the above standard that could benefit from further explanation.

The nature of the breed as described under 'Temperament' is really one of the highlights of the make-up of this thoroughly charming breed. The standard actually states that there should be no tendency toward nervous-

31

ness so one can be reasonably sure that the puppy one buys has a friendly, outgoing character. Were a prospective purchaser to come across a Cavalier without good temperament, however beautiful it looks, it would be sensible to avoid that puppy as clearly the temperament would not fit the breed standard.

The skull of the Cavalier should be almost flat between the ears, not domed as in the King Charles Spaniel or Chihuahua. The stop is the area of indentation between the eyes, where the nasal bone and skull meet, and the length of muzzle is actually specified in the breed standard.

Feathering is mentioned on the ears as well as in the general section under coat. This is the longer fringe of hair upon ears, legs, tail and body, just putting the finishing touches to a Cavalier in good coat.

The mouth of the Cavalier is to have a scissor bite, which means the upper incisors should close tightly over the lower ones. There should not be any significant gap between the upper and lower teeth or the bite would be overshot. Conversely, if the lower incisors overlap the upper ones, a fault that sometimes is found in the breed, this would be a reverse scissor bite. That the standard calls for a complete scissor bite means that the Cavalier should have a full complement of 42 teeth, with six

upper and six lower incisors, these being the smaller teeth set at the front of the mouth between the large canines.

That the body is short-coupled means that the length of body between the end of the rib cage and the pelvic area is not too long, whilst a good spring of rib indicates that the ribs should have a reasonable degree of curvature. They should neither be too flat (known as 'slab-sided'), nor overly rounded (known usually as 'barrelled').

The length of the tail should be in balance with the body. This is one of the reasons why, if the tail is docked, not more than a third of the length is removed. If the tail were too short, it would consequently be out of balance with the rest of the dog. When moving, the tail is carried happily but never carried above the level of the back. The back, incidentally, should be level, meaning that it should not be arched or roached, nor indeed should there be any dip in the back, such that it slopes downwards creating a hollow.

All four recognised colours of the breed should have a long, silky coat that is free from curl, although a slight wave is permissible. Obviously if the coat is very short, or if the texture is too coarse, this would be considered a fault for, when all is said and done, the coat of the Cavalier is its crowning glory.

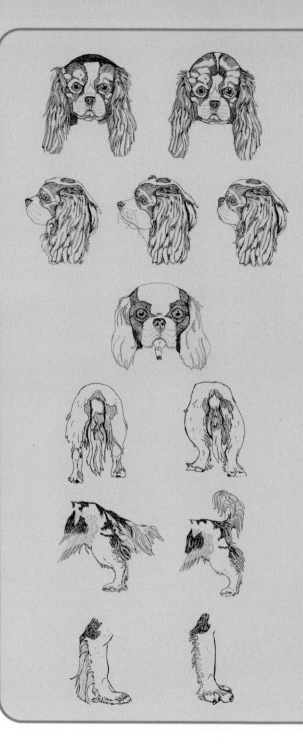

HEAD
The head is almost flat between the ears (left); it should never appear domed (right).

MUZZLE
The muzzle should be about 3.8 cms in length with a shallow stop (left). It should neither be too long (center) nor too short (right).

EYES
The eyes should be large and round but not too prominent.

HINDQUARTERS
The hindquarters have well-turned stifles (left), never turning inward (cowhocks, right).

TAIL
The tail is well set on and carried happily (left), but never much above the level of back (right).

FEET
The feet should be compact and well feathered (left). Toes should not be splayed (right).

Cavalier King Charles Spaniel

Visit the breeder to view the litter and the parents. Surely your child will be happy to help make the selection.

You have probably decided on a Cavalier King Charles Spaniel as your choice of pet following a visit to the home of a friend or acquaintance, where you have seen an adorable Cavalier looking gloriously elegant on the sofa. This certainly makes for a pretty picture, but as a new owner you must realise that a good deal of care, commitment and careful training goes into raising a boisterous puppy so that your pet turns into a well-behaved adult.

In deciding to take on a new puppy, you will be committing yourself to around 12 years of responsibility. No dog should be discarded after a few months or even a few years when the novelty has worn off. Instead, your Cavalier King Charles Spaniel should be joining your household to spend the rest of its days with you.

Although a Cavalier is much easier to look after than many other breeds, you will still need to carry out a certain amount of training. Unlike some of the larger guarding breeds, it will not respond well to overly strict training. Instead you will need to take a firm but gentle approach in order to get the very best out of your pet.

A Cavalier generally likes to be clean around the house, but

DID YOU KNOW?

When breeds become very popular, and such is the case with the Cavalier, although there are many truly dedicated breeders, there become an increasing number of less reputable ones too. It is therefore essential to select a breeder with the very greatest of care.

you will need to teach your puppy what is and is not expected. You will need to be consistent in your instructions; it is no good accepting certain behaviour one day and not the next; your puppy simply will not understand and will be utterly confused. Your Cavalier will want to please you, so you will need to demonstrate clearly how your puppy is to achieve this.

Although the dog you are taking into your home will be fairly small and therefore probably less troublesome than a large dog, there will undoubtedly be a period of settling in. This will be great fun but you must be prepared for mishaps around the home during the first few weeks of your life together. It will be important that precious ornaments are kept well out of harm's way and you will have to think twice about where you place hot cups of coffee or anything breakable. Accidents can and do happen, so you will need to think ahead so as to avoid these. Electric cables must be carefully concealed and your puppy must be taught where and where not to go.

Before making your commitment to a new puppy, do also think carefully about your future holiday plans. Depending on the country in which you live, your dog may or may not be able to travel abroad with you. Because of

quarantine laws, no dog can travel freely in and out of Britain so this must be borne in mind ahead of your purchase. If you have thought things through carefully, discussed the matter thoroughly with all the members of your household, hopefully you will have come to the right decision. If you decide that a Cavalier should join your family this will hopeful-

DID YOU KNOW?
Unfortunately, when a puppy is bought by someone who does not take into consideration the time and attention that dog ownership requires, it is the puppy who suffers when he is either abandoned or placed in a shelter by a frustrated owner. So all of the 'homework' you do in preparation for your pup's arrival will benefit you both. The more informed you are, the more you will know what to expect and the better equipped you will be to handle the ups and downs of raising a puppy. Hopefully, everyone in the household is willing to do his part in raising and caring for the pup. The anticipation of owning a dog often brings a lot of promises from excited family members: 'I will walk him every day,' 'I will feed him,' 'I will housebreak him,' etc., but these things take time and effort, and promises can easily be forgotten once the novelty of the new pet has worn off.

ly be a happy, long-term relationship for all parties concerned.

BUYING THE CAVALIER PUPPY
Although you may be looking for a Cavalier King Charles Spaniel as a pet, rather than a show dog, this does not mean that you want a dog that is in any way 'second-rate'. A caring breeder will have brought up the entire litter of puppies with the same amount of dedication. Thus a puppy destined for a pet home should be just as healthy and outgoing as the one that hopes to end up in the show ring.

Because you have carefully selected this breed, you will want a Cavalier that is a typical

DID YOU KNOW?
Your selection of a good puppy can be determined by your needs. A show potential or a good pet? It is your choice. Every puppy, however, should be of good temperament. Although show-quality puppies are bred and raised with emphasis on physical conformation, responsible breeders strive for equally good temperament. Do not buy from a breeder who concentrates solely on physical beauty at the expense of personality.

DID YOU KNOW?
You should not even think about buying a puppy that looks sick, undernourished, overly frightened or nervous. Sometimes a timid puppy will warm up to you after a 30-minute 'let's-get-acquainted' session.

specimen, both in looks and in temperament. In your endeavours to find such a puppy, you will have to select the breeder with care. The Kennel Club will almost certainly be able to give you names of contacts within Cavalier breed clubs. These people can possibly put you in touch with breeders who may have puppies for sale. However, although these people can point you in the right direction, it will be up to you to do your homework carefully.

Even though you are probably not looking for a show dog, it is always a good idea to visit a show so that you can see quality specimens of the breed. This will also give you an opportunity to meet breeders who will probably be able to answer some of your queries. In addition, you will get some idea about which breeders appear to take most care of their stock, and which are likely to have given their puppies the best possible start in life. Something else you may be able to decide

Select the Cavalier puppy with the temperament and personality that appeal to you. Never buy a dog that appears unhealthy, overly timid or nasty. Fortunately, there are very few temperament concerns in the Cavalier.

upon is which colour appeals to you most, and if you have any other preferences regarding appearance.

When buying your puppy you will need to know about vaccinations, those already given and those still due. It is important that any injections already given by a

veterinary surgeon have documentary evidence to prove this. A worming routine is also vital for any young puppy, so the breeder should be able to tell you exactly what treatment has been given, when it has been administered and how you should continue.

Clearly when selecting a puppy, the one you choose must be in good condition. The coat should look glossy and there should be no discharge from eyes or nose. Ears should also be clean, and of course there should be absolutely no sign of parasites. Check that there is no rash on the skin, and of course the puppy you choose should not have evidence of loose motions.

As in several other breeds, some Cavalier puppies have umbilical hernias, which can be seen as a small lump on the

DID YOU KNOW?

Your puppy should have a well-fed appearance but not a distended abdomen, which may indicate worms or incorrect feeding, or both. The body should be firm, with a solid feel. The skin of the abdomen should be pale pink and clean, without signs of scratching or rash. Check the hind legs to make certain that dewclaws were removed, if any were present at birth.

tummy where the umbilical cord was attached. Clearly it is preferable not to have such a hernia on any puppy, but you should check for this at the outset and if there is one you should discuss the seriousness of this with the breeder. Most umbilical hernias are safe but your vet should keep an eye on this in case an operation is needed.

Finally a few words of warning. Never under any circumstances buy a puppy from a retail outlet, however clean or well managed it may appear. Nor should you buy through a third party, something which happens all too often and may not even be realised by the purchaser. Always insist that you see the puppy's dam and, if possible, the sire. Frequently the sire will not be owned by the breeder of the litter, so a photograph should be available for you to see. Ask if the breeder has any other of the puppy's relations which you could meet; for example there may be an older half-sister or half-brother. It would be beneficial for you to see how they have turned out, their mature size, coat quality, temperament and so on.

Be sure, too, that if you decide to buy a puppy, all relevant sales documentation is provided at the time of sale. You will need a copy of the pedigree, preferably The Kennel Club registration documents, vaccina-

tion certificates and a feeding chart so that you know exactly how the puppy has been fed and how you should continue. Some careful breeders provide their puppy buyers with a small amount of food so that there is no risk of an upset tummy, allowing for a gradual change of diet if that particular brand of food is not locally available.

DID YOU KNOW?

Two important documents you will get from the breeder are the pup's pedigree and registration papers. The breeder should register the litter and each pup with The Kennel Club, and it is necessary for you to have the paperwork if you plan on showing or breeding in the future.

Make sure you know the breeder's intentions on which type of registration he will obtain for the pup. There are limited registrations which may prohibit the dog from being shown or from competing in non-conformation trials such as Working or Agility if the breeder feels that the pup is not of sufficient quality to do so. There is also a type of registration that will permit the dog in non-conformation competition only.

If your dog is registered with a Kennel-Club-recognised breed club, then you can register the pup with The Kennel Club yourself. Your breeder can assist you with the specifics of the registration process.

Who's having more fun...the child or the puppies? If children are going to live with the Cavalier puppy, they should meet before you make the purchase. The way this scene looks, making a selection is going to be very difficult.

COMMITMENT OF OWNERSHIP

After considering all of these factors, you have most likely already made some very important decisions about selecting your puppy. You have chosen a Cavalier King Charles Spaniel, which means that you have decided which characteristics you want in a dog and what type of dog will best fit into your family and lifestyle. If you have selected a breeder, you have gone a step further—you have done your research and found a responsible, conscientious person who breeds quality Cavalier and who should be a reliable source of help as you and your puppy adjust to life together. If you have observed a litter in action, you have obtained a firsthand look at the dynamics of a puppy 'pack' and, thus, you should learn about each pup's individual personality—perhaps you have even found one that particularly appeals to you.

However, even if you have not yet found the Cavalier puppy of your dreams, observing pups will help you learn to recognise

DID YOU KNOW?

Breeders rarely release puppies until they are eight to ten weeks of age. This is an acceptable age for most breeds of dog, excepting toy breeds which are not released until around 12 weeks, given their petite sizes. If a breeder has a puppy that is 12 weeks or more, it is likely well socialised and housetrained. Be sure that it is otherwise healthy before deciding to take it home.

You should always see the dam with her puppies. It is quite usual to select the puppy of your choice when it is still very young and then come to take the puppy home when it is 10 to 12 weeks old.

certain behaviour and to determine what a pup's behaviour indicates about his temperament. You will be able to pick out which pups are the leaders, which ones are less outgoing, which ones are confident, which ones are shy, playful, friendly, aggressive, etc. Equally as important, you will learn to recognise what a healthy pup should look and act like. All of these things will help you in your search, and when you find the Cavalier that was meant for you, you will know it!

Researching your breed, selecting a responsible breeder and observing as many pups as possible are all important steps on the way to dog ownership. It may seem like a lot of effort…and you have not even brought the pup home yet! Remember, though, you cannot be too careful when it comes to deciding on the type of dog you want and finding out about your prospective pup's background. Buying a puppy is not—or should not be—just

DID YOU KNOW?

If you lead an erratic, unpredictable life, with daily or weekly changes in your work requirements, consider the problems of owning a puppy. The new puppy has to be fed regularly, socialised (loved, petted, handled, introduced to other people) and, most importantly, allowed to visit outdoors for toilet training. As the dog gets older, it can be more tolerant of deviations in its feeding and toilet relief.

another whimsical purchase. This is one instance in which you actually do get to choose your own family! You may be thinking that buying a puppy should be fun—it should not be so serious and so much work. Keep in mind that your puppy is not a cuddly stuffed toy or decorative lawn ornament, but a creature that will become a real member of your family. You will come to realise that, whilst buying a puppy is a pleasurable and exciting endeavour, it is not something to be taken lightly. Relax...the fun will start when the pup comes home!

'A baby in a furry disguise' accurately describes this Cavalier angel.

Always keep in mind that a puppy is nothing more than a baby in a furry disguise...a baby who is virtually helpless in a human world and who trusts his owner for fulfilment of his basic needs for survival. In addition to water and shelter, your pup needs care, protection, guidance and love. If you are not prepared to commit to this, then you are not prepared to own a dog.

Wait a minute, you say. How hard could this be? All of my neighbours own dogs and they seem to be doing just fine. Why should I have to worry about all of this? Well, you should not worry about it; in fact, you will probably find that once your Cavalier pup gets used to his new home, he will fall into his place in the family quite naturally. But it never hurts to emphasise the commitment of dog ownership. With some time and patience, it is really not too difficult to raise a curious and exuberant Cavalier pup to be a well-adjusted and well-mannered adult dog—a dog that could be your most loyal friend.

DID YOU KNOW?

If the breeder from whom you are buying a puppy asks you a lot of personal questions, do not be insulted. Such a breeder wants to be sure that you will be a fit provider for his puppy.

41

Durable and portable! Be careful in handling your Cavalier. These three do not seem too disconcerted by their enthusiastic handler.

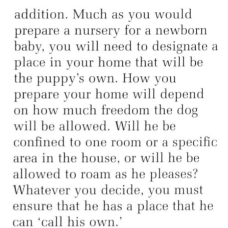

PREPARING PUPPY'S PLACE IN YOUR HOME

Researching your breed and finding a breeder are only two aspects of the 'homework' you will have to do before bringing your Cavalier puppy home. You will also have to prepare your home and family for the new addition. Much as you would prepare a nursery for a newborn baby, you will need to designate a place in your home that will be the puppy's own. How you prepare your home will depend on how much freedom the dog will be allowed. Will he be confined to one room or a specific area in the house, or will he be allowed to roam as he pleases? Whatever you decide, you must ensure that he has a place that he can 'call his own.'

When you bring your new puppy into your home, you are bringing him into what will become his home as well. Obviously, you did not buy a puppy so that he could take over your house, but in order for a puppy to grow into a stable, well-adjusted dog, he has to feel comfortable in his surroundings. Remember, he is leaving the warmth and security of his mother and littermates, as well as the familiarity of the only place he has ever known, so it is important to make his transition as easy as possible. By preparing a place in your home for the puppy, you are making him feel as welcome as possible in a strange new place. It should not take him long to get used to it, but the sudden shock of being transplanted is somewhat traumatic for a young pup. Imagine how a small child would feel in the same situation—that is how your puppy

DID YOU KNOW?

The cost of food must also be mentioned. All dogs need a good quality food with an adequate supply of protein to develop their bones and muscles properly. Most dogs are not picky eaters but unless fed properly they can quickly succumb to skin problems.

42

must be feeling. It is up to you to reassure him and to let him know, 'Little fellow, you are going to like it here!'

WHAT YOU SHOULD BUY
CRATE

To someone unfamiliar with the use of crates in dog training, it may seem like punishment to shut a dog in a crate, but this is not the case at all. Crates are not cruel—crates have many humane and highly effective uses in dog care and training. For example, crate training is a very popular and very successful housebreaking method. A crate can keep your dog safe during travel; and, perhaps most importantly, a crate provides your dog with a place of his own in your home. It serves as a 'doggie bedroom' of sorts—your Cavalier can curl up in his crate when he wants to sleep or when he just needs a break. Many dogs sleep in their crates overnight. When lined with soft blankets and filled with his favourite toys, a crate becomes a cosy pseudo-den for your dog. Like his ancestors, he too will seek out the comfort and retreat of a den—you just happen to be providing him with a safe, clean place to call his own.

As far as purchasing a crate, the type that you buy is up to you. It will most likely be one of the two most popular types: wire or fibreglass. There are advantages and disadvantages to each type.

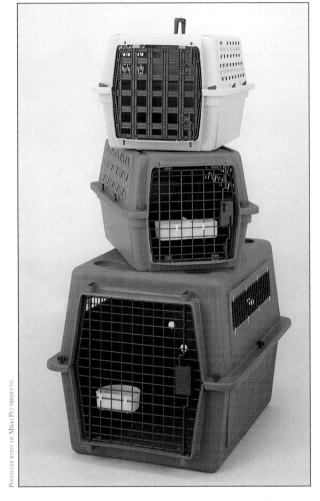

PHOTO COURTESY OF MIKKI PET PRODUCTS.

For example, a wire crate is more open, allowing the air to flow through and affording the dog a view of what is going on around him, whilst a fibreglass crate is sturdier. Both can double as travel crates, providing protection for the dog. The size of the crate is another thing to consider. Puppies do not stay puppies forever but

Your local pet shop should have a variety of crates in various sizes and qualities. A crate is the first thing you should buy for your new puppy.

43

The crate should be large enough to accommodate the Cavalier even after it is fully grown. A medium sized crate is ideal for the Cavalier.

Cavaliers do not increase too greatly in size so you should easily be able to select a crate that will last into adulthood.

BEDDING

Veterinary bedding in the dog's crate will help the dog feel more at home and you ma also pop in a small blanket. This will take the place of the leaves, twigs, etc., that the pup would use in the wild to make a den; the pup can make his own 'burrow' in the crate. Although your pup is far removed from his den-making ancestors, the denning instinct is still a part of his genetic makeup. Secondly, until you bring your pup home, he has been sleeping amidst the warmth of his mother and littermates, and whilst a blanket is not the same as a warm, breathing body, it still provides heat and something with which to snuggle. You will want to wash your pup's blankets frequently in case he has an accident in his crate, and replace or remove any blanket that becomes ragged and starts to fall apart.

Your puppy has just left the warmth of his familiar litter-mates. Don't expect him to adjust to his crate overnight. This is a giant adjustment for such a little creature.

TOYS

Toys are a must for dogs of all ages, especially for curious playful pups. Puppies are the 'children' of the dog world, and what child does not love toys? Chew toys provide enjoyment to both dog and owner—your dog will enjoy playing with his favourite toys, whilst you will enjoy the fact that they distract him from your expensive shoes and leather sofa. Puppies love to chew; in fact, chewing is a physical need for pups as they are teething, and everything looks appetising! The full range of your possessions—from old dishcloth to Oriental rug—are fair game in the eyes of a teething pup. Puppies are not all that discerning when it comes to finding something to literally 'sink their teeth into'—everything tastes great!

Cavalier puppies are fairly aggressive chewers and only the hardest, strongest toys should be offered to them. Breeders advise owners to resist stuffed toys, because they can become de-stuffed in no time. The overly

LEAD

A nylon lead is probably the best option as it is the most resistant to puppy teeth should your pup take a liking to chewing on his lead. Of course, this is a habit that should be nipped in the bud, but if your pup likes to chew on his lead he has a very slim chance of being able to chew through the strong nylon. Nylon leads are also lightweight, which is good for a young Cavalier who is just getting used to the idea of walking on a lead. For everyday walking and safety purposes, the nylon lead is

Bedding is necessary for the crate. As picturesque as this puppy looks, you will have to offer your pup more than leaves to sleep on.

excited pup may ingest the stuffing, which is neither digestible nor nutritious.

Similarly, squeaky toys are quite popular, but must be avoided for the Cavalier. Perhaps a squeaky toy can be used as an aid in training, but not for free play. If a pup 'disembowels' one of these, the small plastic squeaker inside can be dangerous if swallowed. Monitor the condition of all your pup's toys carefully and get rid of any that have been chewed to the point of becoming potentially dangerous.

Be careful of natural bones, which have a tendency to splinter into sharp, dangerous pieces. Also be careful of rawhide, which can turn into pieces that are easy to swallow or into a mushy mess on your carpet.

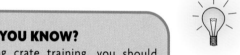

DID YOU KNOW?

During crate training, you should partition off the section of the crate in which the pup stays. If he is given too big an area, this will hinder your training efforts. Crate training is based on the fact that a dog does not like to soil his sleeping quarters, so it is ineffective to keep a pup in a crate that is so big that he can eliminate in one end and get far enough away from it to sleep. Also, you want to make the crate den-like for the pup. Blankets and a favourite toy will make the crate cosy for the small pup; as he grows, you may want to evict some of his 'roommates' to make more room.

It will take some coaxing at first, but be patient. Given some time to get used to it, your pup will adapt to his new home-within-a-home quite nicely.

Cavalier puppies like soft toys. Be sure they are safe toys and only buy your toys at a pet shop.

a good choice. As your pup grows up and gets used to walking on the lead, you may want to purchase a flexible lead. These leads allow you to extend the length to give the dog a broader area to explore or to shorten the length to keep the close to you. Of course there are special leads for training purposes, and specially made leather harnesses for the working Cavaliers, but these are not necessary for routine walks.

COLLAR

Your pup should get used to wearing a collar all the time since you will want to attach his ID tags to it. You have to attach the lead to something! A lightweight nylon collar is a good choice; make sure that it fits snugly enough so that the pup cannot wriggle out of it, but is loose enough so that it will not be uncomfortably tight around the pup's neck. You should be able to fit a finger between the pup and the collar. It may take some time for your pup to get used to wearing the collar, but soon he will not even notice that it is there. Choke collars are made for training, but should only be used by an experienced handler.

FOOD AND WATER BOWLS

Your pup will need two bowls, one for food and one for water. You may want two sets of bowls, one for inside and one for outside,

Rawhide chew bones are very popular and dogs love to chew on them. Always supervise your dog whenever he is chewing on a bone.

46

Your local pet shop should have an interesting variety of toys made especially for dogs. Never use human toys for dogs as they may be dangerous to a puppy.

DID YOU KNOW?

With a big variety of dog toys available, and so many that look like they would be a lot of fun for a dog, be careful in your selection. It is amazing what a set of puppy teeth can do to an innocent-looking toy, so, obviously, safety is a major consideration. Be sure to choose the most durable products that you can find. Hard nylon bones and toys are a safe bet, and many of them are offered in different scents and flavours that will be sure to capture your dog's attention. It is always fun to play a game of catch with your dog, and there are balls and flying discs that are specially made to withstand dog teeth.

depending on where the dog will be fed and where he will be spending most of his time. Stainless steel or sturdy plastic bowls are popular choices. Plastic bowls are more chewable. Dogs tend not to chew on the steel variety, which can be sterilised. It is important to buy sturdy bowls since anything is in danger of being chewed by puppy teeth and you do not want your dog to be constantly chewing apart his bowl (for his safety and for your purse!).

CLEANING SUPPLIES

Until a pup is housetrained you will be doing a lot of cleaning.

47

The buckle collar is the standard collar used for everyday purpose. Be sure that you adjust the buckle on growing puppies. Check it every day. It can become too tight overnight! These collars can be made of leather or nylon. Attach your dog's identification tags to this collar.

The choke chain is the usual collar recommended for training. It is constructed of highly polished steel so that it slides easily through the stainless steel loop. The idea is that the dog controls the pressure around its neck and he will stop pulling if the collar becomes uncomfortable. Never leave a choke collar on your dog when not training.

The halter is for a trained dog that has to be restrained to prevent running away, chasing a cat and the like. Considered the most humane of all collars, it is frequently used on smaller dogs for which collars are not comfortable.

Accidents will occur, which is okay in the beginning because the puppy does not know any better. All you can do is be prepared to clean up any 'accidents.' Old rags, towels, newspapers and a safe disinfectant are good to have on hand.

BEYOND THE BASICS
The items previously discussed are the bare necessities. You will find out what else you need as you go along—grooming supplies, flea/tick protection, baby gates to partition a room, etc. These things will vary depending on your situation but it is important that you have everything you need to feed and make your Cavalier comfortable in his first few days at home.

PUPPY-PROOFING YOUR HOME
Aside from making sure that your Cavalier will be comfortable in your home, you also have to make sure that your home is safe for your Cavalier. This means taking precautions that your pup will not get into anything he should not get into and that there is nothing within his reach that may harm him should he sniff it, chew it, inspect it, etc. This probably seems obvious since, whilst you are primarily concerned with your pup's safety, at the same time you do not want your belongings to be ruined. Breakables should be placed out of reach if your dog is

to have full run of the house. If he is to be limited to certain places within the house, keep any potentially dangerous items in the 'off-limits' areas. An electrical cord can pose a danger should the puppy decide to taste it—and who is going to convince a pup that it would not make a great chew toy? Cords should be fastened tightly against the wall. If your dog is going to spend time in a crate, make sure that there is nothing near his crate that he can reach if he sticks his curious little nose or paws through the openings. Just as you would with a child, keep

Puppies can be more easily trained with the choke chain. These devices control the amount of pressure by their pulling. Never leave the metal choke chain on your Cav. It can damage its coat.

Your pet shop will have a large selection of leads in all colours, materials, lengths, strengths and prices.

DID YOU KNOW?

Grooming tools, collars, leashes, dog beds and, of course, toys will be an expense to you when you first obtain your pup, and the cost will trickle on throughout your dog's lifetime. If your puppy damages or destroys your possessions (as most puppies surely will!) or something belonging to a neighbour, you can calculate additional expense. There is also flea and pest control, which every dog owner faces more than once. You must be able to handle the financial responsibility of owning a dog.

49

all household cleaners and chemicals where the pup cannot get to them.

It is also important to make sure that the outside of your home is safe. Of course your puppy should never be unsupervised, but a pup let loose in the garden will want to run and explore, and he should be granted that freedom. Do not let a fence give you a false sense of security; you would be surprised how crafty (and persistent) a dog can be in figuring out how to dig under and squeeze his way through small holes, or to jump or climb over a fence. The remedy is to make the fence high enough so that it really is impossible for your dog to get over it (about 3 metres should suffice), and well embedded into the ground. Be sure to repair or secure

Cleaning equipment should always be on hand. Yes, you should also clean up droppings left in the garden, especially if people walk in the area which your Cavalier claims as its own.

any gaps in the fence. Check the fence periodically to ensure that it is in good shape and make repairs as needed; a very determined pup may return to the same spot to 'work on it' until he is able to get through.

FIRST TRIP TO THE VET

You have picked out your puppy, and your home and family are ready. Now all you have to do is collect your Cavalier from the breeder and the fun begins, right? Well…not so fast. Something else you need to prepare is your pup's first trip to the veterinary surgeon. Perhaps the breeder can recommend someone in the area that specialises in Cavaliers, or maybe you know some other Cavalier owners who can suggest a good vet. Either way, you should have an appointment arranged for your pup before you pick him up and plan on taking him for an examination before bringing him home.

The pup's first visit will consist of an overall examination to make sure that the pup does not have any problems that are

Opposite page: Your local pet shop will have a large selection of food and water bowls from which you can select the one that best suits your needs.

51

not apparent to the eye. The veterinary surgeon will also set up a schedule for the pup's vaccinations; the breeder will inform you of which ones the pup has already received and the vet can continue from there.

INTRODUCTION TO THE FAMILY

Everyone in the house will be excited about the puppy coming home and will want to pet him and play with him, but it is best to make the introduction low-key so as not to overwhelm the puppy. He is apprehensive already. It is the first time he has been separated from his mother and the breeder, and the ride to your home is likely the first time he

DID YOU KNOW?
It will take at least two weeks for your puppy to become accustomed to his new surroundings. Give him lots of love, attention, handling, frequent opportunities to relieve himself, a diet he likes to eat and a place he can call his own.

has been in an auto. The last thing you want to do is smother him, as this will only frighten him further. This is not to say that human contact is not extremely necessary at this stage, because this is the time when a connection between the pup and his human family is formed. Gentle petting and soothing words should help console him, as well as just putting him down and letting him explore on his own (under your

When offering your Cavalier puppy its first chew bone, make a fuss with soft words of endearment, petting and lots of loving attention.

DID YOU KNOW?
Taking your dog from the breeder to your home in a car can be a very uncomfortable experience for both of you. The puppy will have been taken from his warm, friendly, safe environment and brought into a strange new environment. An environment that moves! Be prepared for loose bowels, urination, crying, whining and even fear biting. With proper love and encouragement when you arrive home, the stress of the trip should quickly disappear.

down to get as close to the pup's level as possible and letting him sniff their hands and petting him gently. He definitely needs human attention and he needs to be touched—this is how to form an immediate bond. Just remember that the pup is experiencing a lot of things for the first time, at the same time. There are new people, new noises, new smells, and new things to investigate: so be gentle, be affectionate, and be as comforting as you can be.

Yes, you should demonstrate your affection for your Cavalier, but kissing on the mouth is not necessary.

YOUR PUP'S FIRST NIGHT HOME

You have travelled home with your new charge safely in his basket or crate. He's been to the vet for a thorough check-over; he's been weighed, his papers examined; perhaps he's even been

watchful eye, of course).

The pup may approach the family members or may busy himself with exploring for a while. Gradually, each person should spend some time with the pup, one at a time, crouching

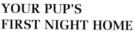

DID YOU KNOW?

You will probably start feeding your pup the same food that he has been getting from the breeder; the breeder should give you a few days' supply to start you off. Although you should not give your pup too many treats, you will want to have puppy treats on hand for coaxing, training, rewards, etc. Be careful, though, as a small pup's calorie requirements are relatively low and a few treats can add up to almost a full day's worth of calories without the required nutrition.

Cavaliers tend to bond closely with one member of the family. They make devoted companions and alert watchdogs as well.

53

You will need a bed and some toys to accommodate your Cavalier on his first night in his new home. Do your best to make the puppy comfortable, but don't overwhelm him all at once.

first night and you are ready to say 'Good night'— keep in mind that this is puppy's first night ever to be sleeping alone. His dam and littermates are no longer at paw's length and he's a bit scared, cold and lonely. Be reassuring to your new family member. This is not the time to spoil him and give in to his inevitable whining.

Puppies whine. They whine to let the others know where they are and hopefully to get company out of it. Place your pup in his new bed or crate in his room and close the door. Mercifully, he may fall asleep without a peep. If the inevitable occurs, ignore the whining: he is fine. Be strong and keep his interest in mind. Do not allow your heart to become guilty and visit the pup. He will fall asleep.

Many breeders recommend placing a piece of bedding from his former homestead in his new bed so that he recognises the scent of his littermates. Others still advise placing a hot water bottle in his bed for warmth. This latter may be a good idea provided the pup doesn't attempt to suckle— he'll get good and wet and may

vaccinated and wormed as well. He's met the family, licked the whole family, including the excited children and the less-than-happy cat. He's explored his area, his new bed, the garden and anywhere else he's been permitted. He's eaten his first meal at home and relieved himself in the proper place. He's heard lots of new sounds, smelled new friends and seen more of the outside world than ever before.

That was just the first day! He's worn out and is ready for bed...or so you think!

It's puppy's

All-day feeders are acceptable for adult dogs that are fully housebroken. Never use these feeders on puppies or on any Cavalier that tends to overeat.

not fall asleep so fast.

Puppy's first night can be somewhat stressful for the pup and his new family. Remember that you are setting the tone of nighttime at your house. Unless you want to play with your pup every evening at 10 p.m.,

midnight and 2 a.m., don't initiate the habit. Your family will thank you, and so will your pup!

PREVENTING PUPPY PROLEMS
SOCIALISATION

Now that you have done all of the preparatory work and have helped your pup get accustomed to his new home and family, it is about time for you to have some fun! Socialising your Cavalier pup gives you the opportunity to show off your new friend, and your pup gets to reap the benefits of being an adorable furry creature that people will want to pet and, in general, think is absolutely precious!

Besides getting to know his new family, your puppy should be exposed to other people, animals and situations, but of course he must not come into close contact with dogs you don't know well until his course of injections is fully completed. This will help him become well adjusted as he grows up and less prone to being timid or fearful of the new things he will encounter. Your pup's socialisation began at the breeder's but now it is your responsibility to continue it. The socialisation he receives up until the age of 12 weeks is the most critical, as this is the time when he forms his impressions of the outside world. Be especially careful during the eight-to-ten-week period, also known as the fear period. The interaction he receives during this time should be gentle and reassuring. Lack of socialisation can manifest itself in fear and aggression as the dog grows up. He needs lots of human

You can always use one of your pillows to make your Cavalier puppy comfortable. The smell of you on the pillow will aid in bonding. Be careful that the puppy doesn't rip the pillow open.

DID YOU KNOW?
Thorough socialisation includes not only meeting new people but also being introduced to new experiences such as riding in the auto, having his coat brushed, hearing the television, walking in a crowd—the list is endless. The more your pup experiences, and the more positive the experiences are, the less of a shock and the less scary it will be for your pup to encounter new things.

Socialisation means getting along with others. The others usually include other dogs, cats and people. This Cavalier and his Rottweiler friend are sharing the same perch.

contact, affection, handling and exposure to other animals.

Once your pup has received his necessary vaccinations, feel free to take him out and about (on his lead, of course). Walk him around the neighbourhood, take him on your daily errands, let people pet him, let him meet other dogs and pets, etc. Puppies do not have to try to make friends; there will be no shortage of people who will want to introduce themselves. Just make sure that you carefully supervise each meeting. If the neighbourhood children want to say hello, for example, that is great—

children and pups most often make great companions. Sometimes an excited child can unintentionally handle a pup too roughly, or an overzealous pup can playfully nip a little too hard. You want to make socialisation experiences positive ones. What a pup learns during this very

It may be best to introduce your Cavalier to other dogs by using a puppy of another breed. The visiting puppy should neither be threatening nor overly dominant.

56

formative stage will impact his attitude toward future encounters. You want your dog to be comfortable around everyone. A pup that has a bad experience with a child may grow up to be a dog that is shy around or aggressive toward children.

CONSISTENCY IN TRAINING
Dogs, being pack animals, naturally need a leader, or else they try to establish dominance in their packs. When you bring a dog into your family, the choice of who becomes the leader and who becomes the 'pack' is entirely up to you! Your pup's intuitive quest for dominance, coupled with the fact that it is nearly impossible to look at an adorable Cavalier pup, with his 'puppy-dog' eyes and not cave in, give the pup almost an unfair advantage in getting the upper hand! A pup will definitely test the waters to see what he can

Pure love and devotion are all the Cavalier knows. Nothing is as rewarding as bonding with your mistress.

and cannot do. Do not give in to those pleading eyes—stand your ground when it comes to disciplining the pup and make sure that all family members do the same. It will only confuse the pup when Mother tells him to get off the couch when he is used to sitting up there with Father to watch the nightly news. Avoid discrepancies by having all members of the household decide on the rules before the pup even comes home…and be consistent in enforcing them! Early training shapes the dog's personality, so you cannot be unclear in what you expect.

COMMON PUPPY PROBLEMS
The best way to prevent puppy problems is to be proactive in stopping an undesirable behaviour as soon as it starts. The

DID YOU KNOW?
An important consideration to be discussed is the sex of your puppy. For a family companion, a bitch may be the better choice, considering the female's inbred concern for all young creatures and her accompanying tolerance and patience. It is always advised to spay a pet bitch, which may guarantee her a longer life.

old saying 'You can't teach an old dog new tricks' does not necessarily hold true, but it is true that it is much easier to discourage bad behaviour in a young developing pup than to wait until the pup's bad behaviour becomes the adult dog's bad habit. There are some problems that are especially prevalent in puppies as they develop.

NIPPING

As puppies start to teethe, they feel the need to sink their teeth into anything available...unfortunately that includes your fingers, arms, hair, and toes. You may find this behaviour cute for the first five seconds...until you feel just how sharp those puppy teeth are. This is something you want to discourage immediately and consistently with a firm 'No!' (or whatever number of firm 'No's' it takes for him to understand that you mean business). Then replace your finger with an appropriate chew toy. Whilst this behaviour is merely annoying when the dog is young, it can become dangerous as your Cavalier's adult teeth grow in and his jaws develop, and he continues to think it is okay to gnaw on human appendages.

CRYING/WHINING

Your pup will often cry, whine, whimper, howl or make some type of commotion when he is left alone. This is basically his way of

DID YOU KNOW?

Chewing goes hand in hand with nipping in the sense that a teething puppy is always looking for a way to soothe his aching gums. In this case, instead of chewing on you, he may have taken a liking to your favourite shoe or something else which he should not be chewing. Again, realise that this is a normal canine behaviour that does not need to be discouraged, only redirected. Your pup just needs to be taught what is acceptable to chew on and what is off limits. Consistently tell him NO when you catch him chewing on something forbidden and give him a chew toy. Conversely, praise him when you catch him chewing on something appropriate. In this way you are discouraging the inappropriate behaviour and reinforcing the desired behaviour. The puppy chewing should stop after his adult teeth have come in, but an adult dog continues to chew for various reasons—perhaps because he is bored, perhaps to relieve tension or perhaps he just likes to chew. That is why it is important to redirect his chewing when he is still young.

calling out for attention to make sure that you know he is there and that you have not forgotten about him. He feels insecure when he is left alone, when you are out of the house and he is in his crate or when you are in another part of the house and he cannot see you. The noise he is making is an expression of the anxiety he feels at being alone, so he needs to be taught that being alone is okay. You are not actually training the dog to stop making noise, you are training him to feel comfortable when he is alone and thus removing the need for him to make the noise. This is where the crate filled with cosy bedding and toys comes in handy. You want to know that he is safe when you are not there to supervise, and you know that he will be safe in his crate rather than roaming freely about the house. In order for the

pup to stay in his crate without making a fuss, he needs to be comfortable in his crate. On that note, it is extremely important that the crate is never used as a form of punishment, or the pup will have a negative association with the crate.

Accustom the pup to the crate in short, gradually increasing time intervals in which you put him in the crate, maybe with a treat, and stay in the room with him. If he cries or makes a fuss, do not go to him, but stay in his sight. Gradually he will realise that staying in his crate is all right without your help, and it will not be so traumatic for him when you are not around. You may want to leave the radio on softly when you leave the house; the sound of human voices may be comforting to him.

DIETARY AND FEEDING CONSIDERATIONS

Today the choices of food for your Cavalier King Charles Spaniel are many and varied. There are simply dozens of brands of food in all sorts of flavours and textures, ranging from puppy diets to those for seniors. There are even hypoallergenic and low-calorie diets available. Because your Cavalier's food has a bearing on coat, health and temperament, it is essential that the most suitable diet is selected for a

Your Cavalier puppy will prosper on a well-balanced diet supplied by the usual dried food. Try feeding your Cav in its crate to encourage it to associate the crate with positive experiences.

Cavalier of his age. It is fair to say, however, that even dedicated owners can be somewhat perplexed by the enormous range of foods available. Only understanding what is best for your dog will help you reach a valued decision.

Dog foods are produced in three basic types: dried, semi-moist and tinned. Dried foods are useful for the cost-conscious for overall they tend to be less expensive than semi-moist or tinned. These contain the least fat and the most preservatives. In general tinned foods are made up of 60—70 percent water, whilst semi-moist ones often contain so much sugar that they are perhaps the least preferred by owners, even though their dogs seem to like them.

When selecting your dog's diet, three stages of development must be considered: the puppy stage, adult stage and the senior or veteran stage.

PUPPY STAGE

Puppies instinctively want to suck milk from their mother's teats and a normal puppy will exhibit this behaviour from just a few moments following birth. If

Cavalier puppies instinctively want to suckle. Mother's milk contains elements that aid the puppy in early resistance to disease.

puppies do not attempt to suckle within the first half-hour or so, they should be encouraged to do so by placing them on a nipple, having selected ones with plenty of milk. This early milk supply is important in providing colostrum to protect the puppies during the first eight to ten weeks of their lives. Although a mother's milk is much better than any milk formula, despite there being some excellent ones available, if the puppies do not feed you will have to feed them yourself. For those with less experience, advice from a veterinary surgeon is important so that you feed not only the right quantity of milk but that of correct quality, fed at suitably frequent intervals, usually every two hours during the first few days of life.

Puppies should be allowed to nurse from their mothers for about the first six weeks, although from the third or fourth week you will have begun to introduce small portions of suitable solid food. Most breeders like to introduce alternate milk and meat meals initially, building up to weaning time.

By the time the puppies are seven or a maximum of eight weeks old, they should be fully weaned and fed solely on a proprietary puppy food. Selection of the most suitable, good-quality diet at this time is essential for a puppy's fastest growth rate is during the first year of life. Veterinary surgeons are usually able to offer advice in this regard and, although the frequency of meals will have been reduced over time, only when a young dog has reached the age of about 18 months should an adult diet be fed.

Puppy and junior diets should be well balanced for the needs of your dog, so that except in certain circumstances additional vitamins, minerals and proteins will not be required.

ADULT DIETS

A dog is considered an adult when it has stopped growing, so in general the diet of a Cavalier can be changed to an adult one at about 10 to 12 months of age.

Again you should rely upon your veterinary surgeon or dietary specialist to recommend an acceptable maintenance diet. Major dog food manufacturers specialise in this type of food, and it is just necessary for you to select the one best suited to your dog's needs. Active dogs may have different requirements than sedate dogs.

SENIOR DIETS

As dogs get older, their metabolism changes. The older dog usually exercises less, moves more slowly and sleeps more. This change in lifestyle and physiological performance requires a change in diet. Since these changes take place slowly, they might not be recognisable. What is easily recognisable is weight gain. By continuing to feed your dog an adult-maintenance diet when it is slowing down metabolically, your dog will gain weight. Obesity in an older dog compounds the health problems that already accompany old age.

As your dog gets older, few of their organs function up to par. The kidneys slow down and the intestines become less efficient. These age-related factors are best handled with a change in diet and a change in feeding schedule to give smaller portions that are more easily digested.

There is no single best diet for every older dog. Whilst many dogs do well on light or senior diets, other dogs do better on puppy diets or other special premium diets such as lamb and rice. Be sensitive to your senior Cavalier's diet and this will help control other problems that may arise with your old friend.

WATER

Just as your dog needs proper nutrition from his food, water is an essential 'nutrient' as well. Water keeps the dog's body properly hydrated and promotes normal function of the body's systems. During housebreaking it is necessary to keep an eye on how much water your Cavalier is drinking, but once he is

DID YOU KNOW?

Many adult diets are based on grain. There is nothing wrong with this as long as it does not contain soy meal. Diets based on soy often cause flatulence (passing gas).

Grain-based diets are almost always the least expensive and a good grain diet is just as good as the most expensive diet containing animal protein.

There are many cases, however, when your dog might require a special diet. These special requirements should only be recommended by your veterinary surgeon.

Read the label on the dog food you are using. Many dog foods only report about half of the contents of the dog food. Become an educated dog owner.

reliably trained he should have access to clean fresh water at all times. Make sure that the dog's water bowl is clean, and change the water often, making sure that water is always available for your dog, especially if you feed dried food.

EXERCISE

Although a Cavalier King Charles Spaniel is small, all dogs require some form of exercise, regardless of breed. A sedentary lifestyle is as harmful to a dog as it is to a person. The Cavalier is a fairly active breed that enjoys exercise, but you don't have to be an Olympic athlete! Regular walks, play sessions in the garden, or letting the dog run free in the garden under your supervision are sufficient forms of exercise for the Cavalier. For those who are more ambitious, you will find that your Cavalier also enjoys long walks, an occasional hike or even a swim! Bear in mind that an overweight dog should never be suddenly over-exercised; instead he should be allowed to increase exercise slowly. Not only is exercise essential to keep the dog's body fit, it is essential to his mental well being. A bored dog will find something to do, which often manifests itself in some type of destructive behaviour. In this sense, it is essential for the owner's mental well being as well!

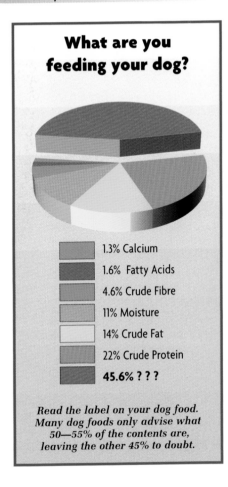

What are you feeding your dog?

1.3% Calcium
1.6% Fatty Acids
4.6% Crude Fibre
11% Moisture
14% Crude Fat
22% Crude Protein
45.6% ? ? ?

Read the label on your dog food. Many dog foods only advise what 50—55% of the contents are, leaving the other 45% to doubt.

GROOMING

Even a Cavalier puppy will need to be groomed regularly so you should train him to enjoy short grooming sessions from a very early age. This will not involve a great deal of time, but ten minutes or so a day should be set aside. It is important that your puppy stands on a solid surface for grooming, a suitable table on which the dog will not slip.

Under no circumstances leave your puppy Cavalier alone on a table for he may all too easily jump off and injure himself.

In adulthood start grooming with your slicker brush, starting from the front and working towards the back of the dog. Leave the face and ears until last. Make sure that you pay particular attention to the areas that are most heavily coated. Always take care not to scratch the skin when grooming and never tug at tangles; instead work at them slowly, just a few hairs at a time and soon enough they will have been eliminated without causing any pain or stress. The coat should then be brushed through with a bristle brush, always checking

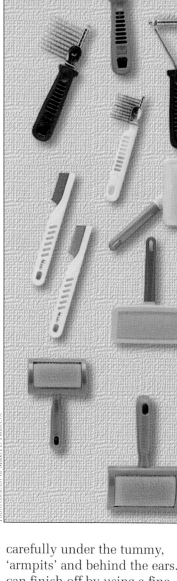

Your local pet shop will have a large supply of grooming tools from which you can choose. Basically, a comb, brush and rake are all that is necessary for the Cavalier's coat.

PHOTO COURTESY OF MIKKI PET PRODUCTS.

DID YOU KNOW?

How much grooming equipment you purchase will depend on how much grooming you are going to do. Here are some basics:

- Natural bristle brush
- Slicker brush
- Metal comb
- Scissors
- Blaster
- Rubber mat
- Dog shampoo
- Spray hose attachment
- Ear cleaner
- Cotton wipes
- Towels
- Nail clippers

carefully under the tummy, 'armpits' and behind the ears. You can finish off by using a fine-toothed comb.

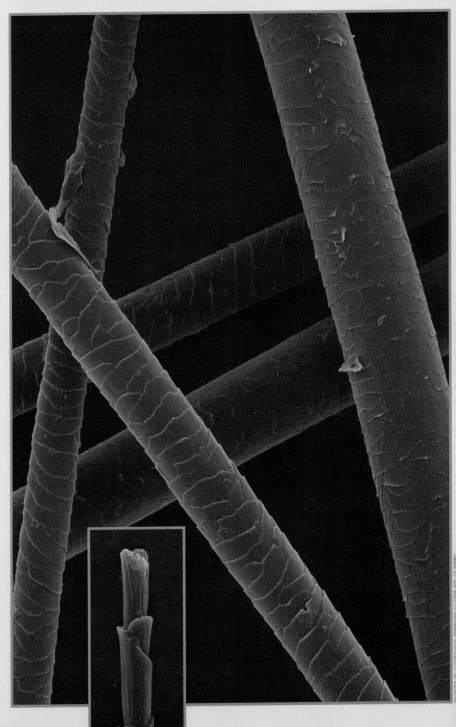

Normal hairs of the Cavalier King Charles Spaniel enlarged 200 times original size. The inset shows the tip of a growing hair enlarged 2000 times its original size. Scanning electron micrographs by Dr Dennis Kunkel, University of Hawaii.

Eyes and mouth should be wiped with a piece of damp cotton wool, tissue or piece of soft lint, then finished with chamois leather or silk. By grooming a little each day, or nearly every day, your Cavalier's coat should never become too problematic and dead hair will be removed as a matter of routine.

BATHING AND DRYING

The frequency with which you bathe your Cavalier will depend to a great extent on whether yours is a show dog or a pet. For the show ring, most exhibitors bathe their dogs before each show, perhaps as frequently as once a week. However, such frequent bathing is by no means essential, provided that the coat has been groomed in between times. The coat should have been groomed through before getting wet, but each owner tends to have his or own tips as to how best to bathe. Personally I always like to stand my dogs on a non-slip mat in the bath and then wet the coat thoroughly using a shower. Always test the temperature of the water beforehand so that it is neither too hot nor too cold. Use a good quality shampoo designed especially for dogs. When this has been thoroughly rinsed off, apply a canine conditioner. You will probably find it best to use a gentler shampoo on the head so as to avoid any irritation to the eyes.

Your Cavalier should be brushed and combed regularly. If you begin grooming your Cav from puppyhood, he should accept grooming naturally as an adult. Be careful not to scratch the dog's skin with the comb.

The feathering parts of the coat should be done with a bristle brush. Always check the armpits, belly and behind the ears for possible matts.

The Cavalier's tail is done with a fine-toothed comb.

67

Check the temperature of the water before wetting your Cav. Use special dog shampoo. Never use human shampoo as it is too strong for a dog's skin.

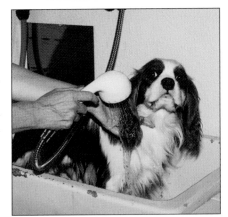

When soaping the dog, be especially carefully around the Cav's eyes and ears. Nothing will convince a Cav that bathes are awful like soap in his eyes and water in his ears!

Use a blaster on low for the final drying process. Be extremely careful not to burn the dog.

It is also a good idea to put pieces of cotton wool in the ears to avoid water getting inside them but do, please, remember to take these out afterwards!

When the coat is completely rinsed through with clean water, you can use highly absorbent cloths to take off excess moisture and then take your dog out of the bath, wrapped in a clean towel. Undoubtedly your Cavalier will want to shake—so be prepared!

Drying can be done on whichever table you use for the grooming process. After a quick brushing, work over the coat systematically with the dryer, again neither too hot nor too cold,

DID YOU KNOW?

Once you are sure that the dog is thoroughly rinsed, squeeze the excess water out of the coat with your hand and dry him with a heavy towel. You may choose to use a blaster on his coat or just let it dry naturally. In cold weather, never allow your dog outside with a wet coat.

There are 'dry bath' products on the market, which are sprays and powders intended for spot cleaning, that can be used between regular baths, if necessary. They are not substitutes for regular baths, but they are easy to use for touch-ups as they do not require rinsing.

so always test it on your hand. You will find that few dogs like air blown directly onto their heads, so leave this until last. Although on a warm day you may be tempted to allow your dog to dry naturally, this will result in the coat curling more than you would wish, apart from which it takes longer so your dog is damp for quite a long while, even on a hot day.

At the end of a bathing session, both you and your Cavalier will be pleased with the results and it is perhaps surprising how enjoyable this procedure can become once you have developed a routine.

EAR CLEANING
The ears should be kept clean and any excess hair inside the ear should be carefully plucked out. Ears can be cleaned with a cotton

DID YOU KNOW?
The use of human soap products like shampoo, bubble bath and hand soap can be damaging to a dog's coat and skin. Human products are too strong and remove the protective oils coating the dog's hair and skin (making him water-resistant). Use only shampoo made especially for dogs and you may like to use a medicated shampoo which will always help to keep external parasites at bay.

Most toy breeds have dental problems, including missing teeth and incorrect bites. Fortunately the Cav is fairly exceptional. Keep a close eye on your Cav's mouth.

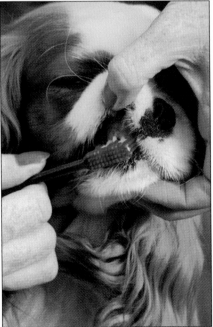

Cleaning your Cavalier's teeth, preferably twice a week, is highly recommended to avoid plaque and tartar buildup.

69

Wrap your wet Cavalier in a heavy towel as soon as you have completed the rinsing phase.

Don't forget to let him shake off! If you don't dry the Cavalier thoroughly, be prepared for a shower all your own!

Ear cleaning should be done regularly. Use a cotton wipe made for ear cleaning and examine the ear for mites. Ear mites are very common and usually cause the dog to scratch its ear frequently.

unusual odour, this is a sure sign of mite infestation or infection and a signal to have his ears checked by the veterinary surgeon.

NAIL CLIPPING

Your Cavalier should be accustomed to having his nails trimmed at an early age, since it will be part of your maintenance routine throughout his life. Not only does it look nicer, but long nails can be sharp if they scratch someone unintentionally. Also, a long nail has a better chance of ripping and bleeding, or causing the feet to spread. A good rule of thumb is that if you can hear your dog's nails' clicking on the floor when he walks, his nails are too long.

Before you start cutting, make sure you can identify the 'quick' in each nail. The quick is a blood vessel that runs through the centre of each nail and grows rather close

wipe and cleaner or ear powder made especially for dogs. Be on the lookout for any signs of infection or ear mite infestation. If your Cavalier has been shaking his head or scratching at his ears frequently, this usually indicates a problem. If his ears have an

to the end. It will bleed if accidentally cut, which will be quite painful for the dog as it contains nerve endings. Keep some type of clotting agent on hand, such as a styptic pencil or styptic powder (the type used for shaving). This will stop the bleeding quickly when applied to the end of the cut nail. Do not panic if this happens, just stop the bleeding and talk soothingly to your dog. Once he has calmed down, move on to the next nail. It is better to clip a little at a time, particularly with black-nailed dogs.

Hold your pup steady as you begin trimming his nails; you do not want him to make any sudden movements or run away. Talk to him soothingly and stroke him as you clip. Holding his foot in your

A sketch of a Cavalier's toe with the nail extending. Cut the tip of the nail only.

If the nail is black, you will be unable to see the quick so use a file to take down the sharp point of the nail.

Light-coloured nails are easier to trim since you can see the quick and avoid cutting it. Few dogs like their nails cut.

DID YOU KNOW?

A dog that spends a lot of time outside on a hard surface such as cement or pavement will have his nails naturally worn down and may not need to have them trimmed as often, except maybe in the colder months when he is not outside as much. Regardless, it is best to get your dog accustomed to this procedure at an early age so that he is used to it. Some dogs are especially sensitive about having their feet touched, but if a dog has experienced it since he was young, he should not be bothered by it

hand, simply take off the end of each nail in one quick clip. You can purchase nail clippers that are specially made for dogs; you can probably find them wherever you buy pet or grooming supplies.

71

Use special dog nail clippers when trimming your Cavalier's nails.

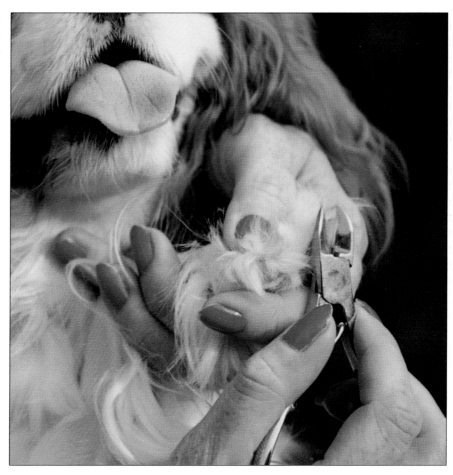

TRAVELLING WITH YOUR DOG
CAR TRAVEL

You should accustom your Cavalier to riding in a car at an early age. You may or may not take him in the car often, but at the very least he will need to go to the vet and you do not want these trips to be traumatic for the dog or a big hassle for you. The safest way for a dog to ride in the car is in his crate. If he uses a crate in the house, you can use the same crate for travel.

Put the pup in the crate and see how he reacts. If he seems uneasy, you can have a passenger hold him on his lap whilst you drive. Another option is a specially made safety harness for dogs, which straps the dog in much like a seat belt. Do not let the dog roam loose in the vehicle—this is very dangerous! If you should stop short, your dog can be thrown and injured. If the dog starts climbing on you and pestering you whilst you are driving, you will not be able to concentrate on the road. It is an unsafe situation for everyone—human and canine.

For long trips, be prepared to stop to let the dog relieve himself. Bring along whatever you need to clean up after him. You should take along some paper kitchen towels and perhaps some old towelling for use should he have an accident in the car or suffer from travel sickness.

AIR TRAVEL

Whilst it is possible to take a dog on a flight within Britain, this is fairly unusual and advance permission is always required. The dog will be required to travel in a fibreglass crate and you should always check in advance with the airline regarding specific requirements. To help the dog be

DID YOU KNOW?
If you are going on a long motor trip with your dog, be sure the hotels are dog friendly. Many hotels do not accept dogs. Also take along some ice that can be thawed and offered to your dog if he becomes overheated. Most dogs like to lick ice.

at ease, put one of his favourite toys in the crate with him. Do not feed the dog for at least six hours before the trip to minimise his need to relieve himself. However, certain regulations specify that

DID YOU KNOW?
When travelling, never let your dog off-lead in a strange area. Your dog could run away out of fear or decide to chase a passing chipmunk or cat or simply want to stretch his legs without restriction—you might never see your canine friend again.

DID YOU KNOW?
Cavalier King Charles Spaniels generally love being in cars and make good travellers. However, as with any breed of dog, some do suffer from travel sickness, but this can easily be remedied by finding a suitable travel-sickness tablet, preferably one recommended by your vet.

water must always be made available to the dog in the crate.

Make sure your dog is properly identified and that your contact information appears on his ID tags and on his crate. Animals travel in a different area of the plane than human passengers so every rule must be strictly adhered to so

Never allow your Cavalier to move freely about your vehicle whilst you are driving. A simple crate is the safest place for the dog during travelling.

as to prevent the risk of getting separated from your dog.

BOARDING

So you want to take a family holiday—and you want to include all members of the family. You would probably make arrangements for accommodations ahead of time

DID YOU KNOW?

For international travel you will have to make arrangements well in advance (perhaps months), as countries' regulations pertaining to bringing in animals differ. There may be special health certificates and/or vaccinations that your dog will need before taking the trip, sometimes this has to be done within a certain time frame. In rabies-free countries, you will need to bring proof of the dog's rabies vaccination and there may be a quarantine period upon arrival.

74

anyway, but this is especially important when travelling with a dog. You do not want to make an overnight stop at the only place around for miles and find out that they do not allow dogs. Also, you do not want to reserve a place for your family without confirming that you are travelling with a dog because if it is against their policy you may not have a place to stay.

DID YOU KNOW?

Never leave your dog alone in the car. In hot weather your dog can die from the high temperature inside a closed vehicle; even a car parked in the shade can heat up very quickly. Leaving the window open is dangerous as well since the dog can hurt himself trying to get out.

Alternatively, if you are travelling and choose not to bring your Cavalier, you will have to make arrangements for him whilst you are away. Some options are to take him to a neighbour's house to stay whilst you are gone, to have a trusted neighbour stop by often or stay at your house, or bring your dog to a reputable boarding kennel. If you choose to board him at a kennel, you should visit in advance to see the facility, how clean it is and where the dogs are kept. Talk to some of the employees and see how they treat the dogs—do they spend time with the dogs, play with them, exercise them, etc.? Also find out the kennel's policy on vaccinations and what they require. This is for all of the dogs' safety, since when dogs are kept together, there is a greater risk of diseases being passed from dog to dog.

DID YOU KNOW?
However much your dog enjoys travelling, he should never be left alone in a car in warm weather, even with the windows left open. Heat builds up all too quickly and can cause suffering and tragedy. Even on a cloudy day one must always be aware that the sun can break through unexpectedly.

A boarding kennel should have ample space for the Cavalier to move about. Inspect the kennel before you use it. Look for cleanliness and the devotion of the staff.

DID YOU KNOW?
The most extensive travel you do with your dog may be limited to trips to the veterinary surgeon's office—or you may decide to bring him along for long distances when the family goes on holiday. Whichever the case, it is important to consider your dog's safety while travelling.

IDENTIFICATION
Your Cavalier is your valued companion and friend. That is why you always keep a close eye on him and you have made sure that he cannot escape from the garden or wriggle out of his collar and run away from you. However, accidents can happen and there may come a time when your dog unexpectedly gets separated from

75

you. If this unfortunate event should occur, the first thing on your mind will be finding him. Proper identification, including an ID tag, a tattoo, and possibly a microchip, will increase the chances of his being returned to you safely and quickly.

Tattooing inhibits the theft and loss of your beloved Cavalier. Some vets perform this service. This photo has been retouched for emphasis.

DID YOU KNOW?

As puppies become more and more expensive, especially those puppies of high quality for showing and/or breeding, they have a greater chance of being stolen. The usual collar dog tag is, of course, easily removed. But there are two techniques that have become widely utilised for identification.

The puppy microchip implantation involves the injection of a small microchip, about the size of a corn kernel, under the skin of the dog. If your dog shows up at a clinic or shelter, or is offered for resale under less than savory circumstances, it can be positively identified by the microchip. The microchip is scanned and a registry quickly identifies you as the owner. This is not only protection against theft, but should the dog run away or go chasing a squirrel and get lost, you have a fair chance of getting it back.

Tattooing is done on various parts of the dog, from its belly to its cheeks. The number tattooed can be your telephone number or any other number which you can easily memorise. When professional dog thieves see a tattooed dog, they usually lose interest in it. Both microchipping and tattooing can be done at your local veterinary clinic. For the safety of our dogs, no laboratory facility or dog broker will accept a tattooed dog as stock.

Your Cavalier should always have a buckle collar with identification tags securely attached.

These Blenheim Cavalier King Charles Spaniels are securely housed by a concrete surface and a heavy gate so they cannot wander away from home and become lost.

77

HOUSEBREAKING AND TRAINING YOUR
Cavalier King Charles Spaniel

Living with an untrained dog is a lot like owning a piano that you do not know how to play—it is a nice object to look at but it does not do much more than that to bring you pleasure. Now try taking piano lessons and suddenly the piano comes alive and brings forth magical sounds and rhythms that set your heart singing and your body swaying.

The same is true with your Cavalier. Any dog is a big responsibility and if not trained sensibly may develop unacceptable behaviour that annoys you or could even cause family friction.

To train your Cavalier, you may like to enrol in an obedience class. Teach him good manners as you learn how and why he behaves the way he does. Find out how to communicate with your dog and how to recognise and understand his communications with you. Suddenly the dog takes on a new role in your life—he is smart, interesting, well

> **DID YOU KNOW?**
> Taking your dog to an obedience school may be the best investment in time and money you can ever make. You will enjoy the benefits for the lifetime of your dog and you will have the opportunity to meet people with your similar expectations for companion dogs.

> **DID YOU KNOW?**
> If you start with a normal, healthy dog and give him time, patience and some carefully executed lessons, you will reap the rewards of that training for the life of the dog. And what a life it will be! The two of you will find immeasurable pleasure in the companionship you have built together with love, respect and understanding. Good luck and enjoy!

behaved and fun to be with. He demonstrates his bond of devotion to you daily. In other words, your Cavalier does wonders for your ego because he constantly reminds you that you are not only his leader, you are his hero!

Those involved with teaching dog obedience and counselling owners about their dogs' behaviour have discovered some interesting facts about dog ownership. For example, training dogs when they are puppies results in the highest

If you are attempting to train an older dog, you must accept the dog's slower rate of learning. Treats are a great assistance for puppy or dog alike.

rate of success in developing well-mannered and well-adjusted adult dogs. Training an older dog, from six months to six years of age, can produce almost equal results providing that the owner accepts the dog's slower rate of learning capability and is willing to work patiently to help the dog succeed at developing to his fullest potential. Unfortunately, many owners of untrained adult dogs lack the patience factor, so they do not persist until their dogs are successful at learning particular behaviours.

Training a puppy aged 10 to 16 weeks (20 weeks at the most) is like working with a dry sponge in a pool of water. The pup soaks up whatever you show him and constantly looks for more things to do and learn. At this early age, his body is not yet producing hormones, and therein lies the reason for such a high rate of success. Without hormones, he is focused on his owners and not particularly interested in investigating other places, dogs, people, etc. You are his leader: his provider of food, water, shelter and security. He latches onto you and wants to stay close. He will usually follow you from room to room, will not let you out of his sight when you are outdoors with him, and respond in

DID YOU KNOW?
Training a dog is a life experience. Many parents admit that much of what they know about raising children they learned from caring for their dogs. Dogs respond to love, fairness and guidance, just as children do. Become a good dog owner and you may become an even better parent.

curiosity emerges and he begins to investigate the world around him. It is at this time when you may notice that the untrained dog begins to wander away from you and even ignore your commands to stay close. When this behaviour becomes a problem, the owner has two choices: get rid of the dog or train him. It is strongly urged that you choose the latter option.

There are usually classes within a reasonable distance from

like manner to the people and animals you encounter. If you greet a friend warmly, he will be happy to greet the person as well. If, however, you are hesitant, even anxious, about the approach of a stranger, he will respond accordingly.

Once the puppy begins to produce hormones, his natural

the owner's home, but you also do a lot to train your dog yourself. Sometimes there are classes available but the tuition is too costly. Whatever the circumstances, the solution to the problem of lack of lesson availability lies within the pages of this book.

This chapter is devoted to helping you train your Cavalier at home. If the recommended procedures are followed faithfully, you may expect positive results that will prove rewarding to both you and your dog.

Whether your new charge is a puppy or a mature adult, the methods of teaching and the techniques we use in training basic behaviours are the same. After all, no dog, whether puppy or adult, likes harsh or inhumane methods. All creatures, however, respond favourably to gentle motivational methods and sincere praise and encouragement. Now let us get started.

DID YOU KNOW?

Occasionally, a dog and owner who have not attended formal classes have been able to earn entry-level titles by obtaining competition rules and regulations from a local kennel club and practising on their own to a degree of perfection. Obtaining the higher level titles, however, almost always requires extensive training under the tutelage of experienced instructors. In addition, the more difficult levels require more specialised equipment whereas the lower levels do not.

When puppies are led to soft grass, their natural instinct is to relieve themselves. They may sniff around in search of an area already utilised by a different dog.

HOUSEBREAKING

You can train a puppy to relieve itself wherever you choose, but this must be somewhere suitable. You should bear in mind from the outset that when your puppy is old enough to go out in public places, any canine deposits must be removed at once. You will always have to carry with you a small plastic bag or 'poop-scoop.'

Outdoor training includes such surfaces as grass, dirt and cement. Indoor training usually means training your dog to newspaper.

When deciding on the surface and location that you will want your Cavalier to use, be sure it is going to be permanent. Training your dog to grass and then changing your mind two months later is extremely

When deciding on the surface of your Cav's relief area, be consistent. Cavaliers can be trained on grass, newspaper, cat litter, sand or something hard like slate or concrete. But once trained, they search for this same substrata to serve their needs.

difficult for both dog and owner.

Next, choose the command you will use each and every time you want your puppy to void. 'Go hurry up' and 'Toilet' are examples of

commands commonly used by dog owners.

Get in the habit of giving the puppy your chosen relief command before you take him out. That way, when he becomes an adult, you will be able to determine if he wants to go out when you ask him. A confirmation will be signs of interest, wagging his tail, watching you intently, going to the door, etc.

PUPPY'S NEEDS

Puppy needs to relieve himself after play periods, after each meal, after he has been sleeping and any time he indicates that he is looking for a

After every nap, be sure the Cav puppy finds his way to his designated relief area.

place to urinate or defecate.

The urinary and intestinal tract muscles of very young puppies are not fully developed. Therefore, like human babies, puppies need to relieve themselves frequently.

Take your puppy out often—every hour for an eight-week-old, for example, and always immediately after sleeping and eating. The older the puppy, the less often he will need to relieve himself. Finally, as a mature healthy adult, he will require only three to five relief trips per day.

HOUSING

Since the types of housing and control you provide for your puppy has a direct relationship on the success of housetraining, we consider the various aspects of both before we begin training.

Bringing a new puppy home and turning him loose in your house can be compared to turning a child loose in a sports arena and telling the child that the place is all his! The sheer enormity of the place would

be too much for him to handle.

Instead, offer the puppy clearly defined areas where he can play, sleep, eat and live. A room of the house where the family gathers is the most obvious choice. Puppies are social animals and need to feel a part of the pack right from the start. Hearing your voice, watching you whilst you are doing things and smelling you nearby are all positive reinforcers that he is now a member

Canine Development Schedule

It is important to understand how and at what age a puppy develops into adulthood. If you are a puppy owner, consult the following Canine Development Schedule to determine the stage of development your Cavalier King Charles Spaniel puppy is currently experiencing. This knowledge will help you as you work with the puppy in the weeks and months ahead.

Period	Age	Characteristics
FIRST TO THIRD	BIRTH TO SEVEN WEEKS	Puppy needs food, sleep and warmth, and responds to simple and gentle touching. Needs mother for security and disciplining. Needs littermates for learning and interacting with other dogs. Pup learns to function within a pack and learns pack order of dominance. Begin socialising with adults and children for short periods. Begins to become aware of its environment.
FOURTH	EIGHT TO TWELVE WEEKS	Brain is fully developed. Needs socialising with outside world. Remove from mother and littermates. Needs to change from canine pack to human pack. Human dominance necessary. Fear period occurs between 8 and 16 weeks. Avoid fright and pain.
FIFTH	THIRTEEN TO SIXTEEN WEEKS	Training and formal obedience should begin. Less association with other dogs, more with people, places, situations. Period will pass easily if you remember this is pup's change-to-adolescence time. Be firm and fair. Flight instinct prominent. Permissiveness and over-disciplining can do permanent damage. Praise for good behaviour.
JUVENILE	FOUR TO EIGHT MONTHS	Another fear period about 7 to 8 months of age. It passes quickly, but be cautious of fright and pain. Sexual maturity reached. Dominant traits established. Dog should understand sit, down, come and stay by now.

NOTE: THESE ARE APPROXIMATE TIME FRAMES. ALLOW FOR INDIVIDUAL DIFFERENCES IN PUPPIES.

DID YOU KNOW?
The golden rule of dog training is simple. For each 'question' (command), there is only one correct answer (reaction). One command = one reaction. Keep practising the command until the dog reacts correctly without hesitating. Be repetitive but not monotonous. Dogs get bored just as people do!

Wire crates have their value over fibreglass crates. They are usually inexpensive and lightweight. They also provide more visual contact between you and the puppy. Cavs like to look around.

so. In those cases, they then become dirty dogs and usually remain that way for life.

The designated area should be lined with clean bedding and a toy. Water must always be available, in a non-spill container.

CONTROL
By control, we mean helping the puppy to create a lifestyle pattern that will be compatible to that of his human pack (YOU!). Just as we guide little children to learn our way of life,

of your pack. Usually a family room, the kitchen or a nearby adjoining breakfast area is ideal for providing safety and security for both puppy and owner.

Within that room there should be a smaller area which the puppy can call his own. An alcove, a wire or fibreglass dog crate or a fenced (not boarded!) corner from which he can view the activities of his new family will be fine. The size of the area or crate is the key factor here. The area must be large enough for the puppy to lie down and stretch out as well as stand up without rubbing his head on the top, yet small enough so that he cannot relieve himself at one end and sleep at the other without coming into contact with his droppings until fully trained to relieve himself outside.

Dogs are, by nature, clean animals and will not remain close to their relief areas unless forced to do

DID YOU KNOW?
A basic obedience beginner's class usually lasts for six to eight weeks. Dog and owner attend an hour-long lesson once a week and practice for a few minutes, several times a day, each day at home. If done properly, the whole procedure will result in a well-mannered dog and an owner who delights in living with a pet that is eager to please and enjoys doing things with his owner.

we must show the puppy when it is time to play, eat, sleep, exercise and even entertain himself.

Your puppy should always sleep in his crate. He should also learn that, during times of household confusion and excessive human activity such as at breakfast when family members are preparing for the day, he can play by himself in relative safety and comfort in his designated area. Each time you leave the puppy alone, he should understand exactly where he is to stay. Puppies are chewers. They cannot tell the difference between lamp cords, television wires, shoes, table legs, etc. Chewing into a television wire, for example, can be fatal to the puppy whilst a shorted wire

DID YOU KNOW?
Practice Makes Perfect!
- Have training lessons with your dog every day in several short segments—three to five times a day for a few minutes at a time is ideal.
- Do not have long practice sessions. The dog will become easily bored.
- Never practice when you are tired, ill, worried or in an otherwise negative mood. This will transmit to the dog and may have an adverse effect on its performance.

Think fun, short and above all POSITIVE! End each session on a high note, rather than a failed exercise, and make sure to give a lot of praise. Enjoy the training and help your dog enjoy it, too.

DID YOU KNOW?
Do not carry your dog to his toilet area. Lead him there on a leash or, better yet, encourage him to follow you to the spot. If you start carrying him to his spot, you might end up doing this routine forever and your dog will have the satisfaction of having trained YOU.

can start a fire in the house.

If the puppy chews on the arm of the chair when he is alone, you will probably discipline him angrily when you get home. Thus, he makes the association that your coming home means he is going to be punished. (He will not remember chewing up the chair and is incapable of making the association of the discipline with his naughty deed.)

Other times of excitement, such as family parties, etc., can be fun for the puppy providing he can view the activities from the security of his designated area. He is not underfoot and he is not being fed all sorts of titbits that will probably cause him stomach distress, yet he still feels a part of the fun.

SCHEDULE

A puppy should be taken to his relief area each time he is released from his designated area, after meals, after a play session, when he first

THE SUCCESS METHOD
6 Steps to Successful Crate Training

1 Tell the puppy 'Crate time!' and place him in the crate with a small treat (a piece of cheese or half of a biscuit). Let him stay in the crate for five minutes while you are in the same room. Then release him and praise lavishly. Never release him when he is fussing. Wait until he is quiet before you let him out.

2 Repeat Step 1 several times a day.

3 The next day, place the puppy in the crate as before. Let him stay there for ten minutes. Do this several times.

4 Continue building time in five-minute increments until the puppy stays in his crate for 30 minutes with you in the room. Always take him to his relief area after prolonged periods in his crate.

5 Now go back to Step 1 and let the puppy stay in his crate for five minutes, this time while you are out of the room.

6 Once again, build crate time in five-minute increments with you out of the room. When the puppy will stay willingly in his crate (he may even fall asleep!) for 30 minutes with you out of the room, he will be ready to stay in it for several hours at a time.

DID YOU KNOW?

Most of all, be consistent. Always take your dog to the same location, always use the same command, and always have him on lead when he is in his relief area, unless a fenced-in garden is available.

By following the Success Method, your puppy will be completely housetrained by the time his muscle and brain development reach maturity. Keep in mind that small breeds usually mature faster than large breeds, but all puppies should be trained by six months of age.

awakens in the morning (at age eight weeks, this can mean 5 a.m.!). The puppy will indicate that he's ready 'to go' by circling or sniffing busily—-do not misinterpret these signs. For a puppy less than ten weeks of age, a routine of taking him out every hour is necessary. As the puppy grows, he will be able to wait for longer periods of time.

Keep trips to his relief area short. Stay no more than five or six minutes and then return to the house. If he goes during that time, praise him lavishly and take him indoors immediately. If he does not, but he has an accident when you go

HOW MANY TIMES A DAY?

AGE	RELIEF TRIPS
To 14 weeks	10
14–22 weeks	8
22–32 weeks	6
Adulthood	4
(dog stops growing)	

These are estimates, of course, but they are a guide to the MINIMUM opportunities a dog should have each day to relieve itself.

Help him develop regular hours for naps, being alone, playing by himself and just resting, all in his crate. Encourage him to entertain himself whilst you are busy with your activities. Let him learn that having you near is comforting, but it is not your main purpose in life to provide him with undivided attention.

Each time you put a puppy in his own area, use the same command, whatever suits best. Soon, he will run to his crate or special area when he hears you say those words.

Crate training provides safety for you, the puppy and the home. It also provides the puppy with a feeling of security, and that helps the puppy achieve self-confidence and clean habits.

Remember that one of the primary ingredients in housetraining your puppy is control. Regardless of your lifestyle, there will always be

back indoors, pick him up immediately, say 'No! No!' and return to his relief area. Wait a few minutes, then return to the house again. never hit a puppy or rub his face in urine or excrement when he has an accident!

Once indoors, put the puppy in his crate until you have had time to clean up his accident. Then release him to the family area and watch him more closely than before. Chances are, his accident was a result of your not picking up his signal or waiting too long before offering him the opportunity to relieve himself. Never hold a grudge against the puppy for accidents.

Let the puppy learn that going outdoors means it is time to relieve himself, not play. Once trained, he will be able to play indoors and out and still differentiate between the times for play versus the times for relief.

Your Cavalier puppy is easily trained to know that going outside means relief time.

occasions when you will need to have a place where your dog can stay and be happy and safe. Training is the answer for now and in the future.

In conclusion, a few key elements are really all you need for a successful house training method—consistency, frequency, praise, control and supervision. By following these procedures with a normal, healthy puppy, you and the puppy will soon be past the stage of 'accidents' and ready to move on to a full and rewarding life together.

ROLES OF DISCIPLINE, REWARD AND PUNISHMENT

Discipline, training one to act in accordance with rules, brings order to life. It is as simple as that. Without discipline, particularly in a group society, chaos reigns supreme

and the group will eventually perish. Humans and canines are social animals and need some form of discipline in order to function effectively. They must procure food, protect their home base and their young and reproduce to keep the species going.

If there were no discipline in the lives of social animals, they would eventually die from starvation and/or predation by other stronger animals.

In the case of domestic canines,

Be careful never to leave your Cavalier crated whilst outdoors in the sun. A dog can suffer heatstroke quite readily so an owner must be very cautious.

You should make a habit of cleaning up your dog's droppings wherever they may be. Handy sanitation devices are available at most pet shops to make this chore easier.

DID YOU KNOW?

By providing sleeping and resting quarters that fit the dog, and offering frequent opportunities to relieve himself outside his quarters, the puppy quickly learns that the outdoors (or the newspaper if you are training him to paper) is the place to go when he needs to urinate or defecate. It also reinforces his innate desire to keep his sleeping quarters clean. This, in turn, helps develop the muscle control that will eventually produce a dog with clean living habits.

dogs need discipline in their lives in order to understand how their pack (you and other family members) functions and how they must act in order to survive.

A large humane society in a highly populated area recently surveyed dog owners regarding their satisfaction with their relationships with their dogs. People who had trained their dogs were 75% more satisfied with their pets than those who had never trained their dogs.

Dr. Edward Thorndike, a psychologist, established *Thorndike's Theory of Learning*, which states that a behaviour that results in a pleasant event tends to be repeated. A behaviour that results in an unpleasant event tends not to be repeated. It is this theory on which training methods are based today. For example, if you manipulate a dog to perform a specific behaviour and reward him for doing it, he is likely to do it again because he enjoyed the end result.

Occasionally, punishment, a penalty inflicted for an offence, is necessary. The best type of punishment often comes from an outside source. For example, a child is told not to touch the stove because he may get burned. He disobeys and touches the stove. In doing so, he receives a burn. From that time on, he respects the heat of the stove and avoids contact with it. Therefore, a behaviour that results in an unpleasant event tends not to be repeated.

A good example of a dog learning the hard way is the dog who chases the house cat. He is told many times to leave the cat alone, yet he persists in teasing the cat. Then, one day he begins chasing the cat but the cat turns and swipes a claw across the dog's face, leaving him with a painful gash on his nose. The final result is that the dog stops chasing the cat.

TRAINING EQUIPMENT
COLLAR AND LEAD
For a Cavalier the collar and lead that you use for training must be one with which you are easily able to work, not too heavy for the dog and perfectly safe.

DID YOU KNOW?

The puppy should also have regular play and exercise sessions when he is with you or a family member. Exercise for a very young puppy can consist of a short walk around the house or garden. Playing can include fetching games with a large ball or a special raggy. (All puppies teethe and need soft things upon which to chew.) Remember to restrict play periods to indoors within his living area (the family room for example) until he is completely housetrained.

TREATS

Have a bag of treats on hand. Something nutritious and easy to swallow works best. Use a soft treat, a chunk of cheese or a piece of cooked chicken rather than a dry biscuit. By the time the dog gets done chewing a dry treat, he will forget why he is being rewarded in the first place! Using food rewards will not teach a dog to beg at the table—the only way to teach a dog to beg at the table is to give him food from the table. In training, rewarding the dog with a food treat will help him associate praise and the treats with learning new behaviours that obviously please his owner.

TRAINING BEGINS: ASK THE DOG A QUESTION

In order to teach your dog anything, you must first get his attention. After all, he cannot learn anything if he is looking away from you with his mind on something else.

To get his attention, ask him, 'School?' and immediately walk over to him and give him a treat as you tell him 'Good dog.' Wait a minute or two and repeat the routine, this time with a treat in your hand as you approach within a foot of the dog. Do not go directly to him, but stop about a foot short of him and hold out the treat as you ask, 'School?' He will see you approaching with a treat in your hand and most likely begin walking toward you. As you meet, give him the treat and praise again.

The third time, ask the question, have a treat in your hand and walk only a short distance toward the dog so that he must walk almost all the way to you. As he reaches you, give him the treat and praise again.

By this time, the dog will probably be getting the idea that if he pays attention to you, especially when you ask that question, it will pay off in treats and

DID YOU KNOW?

If you want to be successful in training your dog, you have four rules to obey yourself:

1. Develop an understanding of how a dog thinks.
2. Do not blame the dog for lack of communication.
3. Define your dog's personality and act accordingly.
4. Have patience and be consistent.

fun activities for him. In other words, he learns that 'school' means doing fun things with you that result in treats and positive attention for him.

Remember that the dog does not understand your verbal language, he only recognises sounds. Your question translates to a series of sounds for him, and those sounds become the signal to go to you and pay attention; if he does, he will get to interact with you plus receive treats and praise.

THE BASIC COMMANDS
TEACHING SIT

Now that you have the dog's attention, attach his lead and hold it in your left hand and a food treat in your right. Place your food hand at the dog's nose and let him lick the treat but not take it from you. Say 'Sit' and slowly raise your food hand from in front of the dog's nose up over his head so that he is looking at the ceiling. As he bends his head upward, he will have to bend his knees to maintain his balance. As he bends his knees, he will assume a sit position. At that point, release the food treat and praise lavishly with comments such as 'Good dog! Good sit!', etc. Remember to always praise enthusiastically, because dogs relish verbal

DID YOU KNOW?

Never train your dog, puppy or adult, when you are mad or in a sour mood. Dogs are very sensitive to human feelings, especially anger, and if your dog senses that you are angry or upset, he will connect your anger with his training and learn to resent or fear his training sessions.

praise from their owners and feel so proud of themselves whenever they accomplish a behaviour.

You will not use food forever in getting the dog to obey your commands. Food is only used to teach new behaviours, and once the dog knows what you want when you give a specific command, you will wean him off of the food treats but still maintain the verbal praise.

Training your Cavalier to 'Sit' is an easy task. Use the food treat to keep the dog's attention.

DID YOU KNOW?

Dogs do not understand our language. They can be trained to react to a certain sound, at a certain volume. If you say 'No, Oliver' in a very soft pleasant voice it will not have the same meaning as 'No, Oliver!!' when you shout it as loud as you can. You should never use the dog's name during a reprimand, just the command NO!! Since dogs don't understand words, comics use dogs trained with opposite meanings. Thus, when the comic commands his dog to SIT the dog will stand up; and vice versa.

DID YOU KNOW?

Dogs are as different from each other as people are. What works for one dog may not work for another. Have an open mind. If one method of training is unsuccessful, try another.

Once your Cavalier has learned to obey your 'Sit' command, start to move away from him slowly repeating the 'Sit' command. This is the beginning of the 'Stay' training.

After all, you will always have your voice with you, and there will be many times when you have no food rewards but expect the dog to obey.

TEACHING DOWN

Teaching the down exercise is easy when you understand how the dog perceives the down position, and it is very difficult when you do not. Dogs perceive the down position as a submissive one, therefore teaching the down exercise using a forceful method can sometimes make the dog develop such a fear of the down that he either runs away when you say 'Down' or he attempts to snap at the person who tries to force him down.

Have the dog sit close alongside your left leg, facing in the same direction as you are. Hold the lead in your left hand and a food treat in your right. Now place your left hand lightly on the top of the dog's shoulders where they meet above the spinal cord. Do not push down on the dog's shoulders; simply rest your left hand there so you can guide the dog to lie down close to your left leg rather than to swing away from your side when he drops.

Now place the food hand at the dog's nose, say 'Down' very softly (almost a whisper), and slowly lower the food hand to the dog's front feet. When the food hand reaches the floor, begin moving it forward along the floor in front of the dog. Keep talking softly to the dog, saying things like, 'Do you want this treat? You can do this, good dog.' Your reassuring tone of voice will help

DID YOU KNOW?

A dog in jeopardy never lies down. He stays alert on his feet because instinct tells him that he may have to run away or fight for his survival. Therefore, if a dog feels threatened or anxious, he will not lie down. Consequently, it is important to have the dog calm and relaxed as he learns the down exercise.

calm the dog as he tries to follow the food hand in order to get the treat.

When the dog's elbows touch the floor, release the food and praise softly. Try to get the dog to maintain that down position for several

The 'Down' position is not a natural one for dogs. In their own world, dogs lie down in fear or submission, and in repose. Using a gentle approach (and a tasty morsel), you can convince your Cav that 'Down' is a good place to be.

seconds before you let him sit up again. The goal here is to get the dog to settle down and not feel threatened in the down position.

TEACHING STAY

It is easy to teach the dog to stay in either a sit or a down position. Again, we use food and praise during the teaching process as we help the dog to understand exactly what it is that we are expecting him to do.

To teach the sit/stay, start with the dog sitting on your left side as before and hold the lead in your left hand. Have a food treat in your right hand and place your food hand at the dog's nose. Say 'Stay' and step out on your right foot to stand directly in front of the dog, toe to toe, as he licks and nibbles the treat. Be sure to keep his head facing

upward to maintain the sit position. Count to five and then swing around to stand next to the dog again with him on your left. As soon as you get back to the original position, release the food and praise lavishly.

To teach the down/stay, do the down as previously described. As soon as the dog lies down, say 'Stay' and step out on your right foot just as you did in the sit/stay. Count to five and then return to stand beside the dog with him on your left side. Release the treat and praise as always.

Within a week or ten days, you can begin to add a bit of distance between you and your dog when you leave him. When you do, use your left hand open with the palm facing the dog as a stay signal, much the same as the hand signal a police officer uses to stop traffic at an intersection. Hold the food treat in your right hand as before, but this time the food is not touching the dog's nose. He will watch the food hand and quickly learn that he is going to get that treat as soon as you return to his side.

When you can stand 1 metre away from your dog for 30 seconds, you can then begin building time and distance in both stays. Eventually, the dog can be expected to remain in the stay position for prolonged periods of time until you return to him or call him to you. Always praise when he stays.

TEACHING COME

If you make teaching 'come' a fun experience, you should never have a 'student' that does not love the game or that fails to come when called. The secret, it seems, is never to teach the word 'come.'

At times when an owner most wants his dog to come when called, the owner is likely upset or anxious and he allows these feelings to come through in the tone of his voice when he calls his dog. Hearing that desperation in his owner's voice, the dog fears the results of going to him

> **DID YOU KNOW?**
>
> When calling the dog, do not say 'Come.' Say things like, 'Rover, where are you? See if you can find me! I have a cookie for you!' Keep up a constant line of chatter with coaxing sounds and frequent questions such as, 'Where are you?' The dog will learn to follow the sound of your voice to locate you and receive his reward.

dog, and each person should celebrate the dog's finding him with a treat and lots of happy praise. When a person calls the dog, he is actually inviting the dog to find him and get a treat as a reward for 'winning.'

A few turns of the 'Where are you?' game and the dog will figure out that everyone is playing the game and that each person has a big celebration awaiting his success at locating them. Once he learns to love the game, simply calling out 'Where are you?' will bring him running from wherever he is when he hears that all-important question.

The come command is recognised as one of the most important things to teach a dog, but there are trainers who work with thousands of dogs and never teach the actual word 'Come.' Yet these dogs will race to respond to a person who uses the dog's name followed by 'Where are you?' For example, a

Always speak in a happy tone of voice when calling your Cavalier to you. If he senses that you're anxious or angry, he will hesitate to come near you.

and therefore either disobeys outright or runs in the opposite direction. The secret, therefore, is to teach the dog a game and, when you want him to come to you, simply play the game. It is practically a no-fail solution!

To begin, have several members of your family take a few food treats and each go into a different room in the house. Take turns calling the

woman has a 12-year-old companion dog who went blind, but who never fails to locate her owner when asked, 'Where are you?'

Children particularly love to play this game with their dogs. Children can hide in smaller places like a shower or bathtub, behind a bed or under a table. The dog needs to work a little bit harder to find these hiding places, but when he does he loves to celebrate with a treat and a tussle with a favourite youngster.

TEACHING HEEL

Heeling means that the dog walks beside the owner without pulling. It takes time and patience on the owner's part to succeed at teaching the dog that he (the owner) will not proceed unless the dog is walking calmly beside him. Pulling out ahead on the lead is definitely not acceptable.

DID YOU KNOW?
Never call your dog to come to you for a correction or scold him when he reaches you. That is the quickest way to turn a 'Come' command into 'Go away fast!' Dogs think only in the present tense and he will connect the scolding with coming to his master, not with the misbehaviour of a few moments earlier.

DID YOU KNOW?
Play fetch games with your puppy in an enclosed area where he can retrieve his toy and bring it back to you. Always use a toy or object designated just for this purpose. Never use a shoe, sock or other item he may later confuse with those in your closet or underneath your chair.

Begin with holding the lead in your left hand as the dog sits beside your left leg. Move the loop end of the lead to your right hand but keep your left hand short on the lead so it keeps the dog in close next to you.

Say 'Heel' and step forward on your left foot. Keep the dog close to you and take three steps. Stop and have the dog sit next to you in what we now call the 'heel position.' Praise verbally, but do not touch the dog. Hesitate a moment and begin again with 'Heel,' taking three steps and stopping, at which point the dog is told to sit again.

Your goal here is to have the dog walk those three steps without pulling on the lead. When he will walk calmly beside you for three steps without pulling, increase the number of steps you take to five. When he will walk politely beside you whilst you take five steps, you can increase the length of your walk to ten steps. Keep increasing the length of your stroll until the dog

DID YOU KNOW?
If you begin teaching the heel by taking long walks and letting the dog pull you along, he misinterprets this action as an acceptable form of taking a walk. When you pull back on the lead to counteract his pulling, he reads that tug as a signal to pull even harder!

Teaching your dog to 'Heel' begins with the dog in a sitting position. Cavaliers are easy to train because they are so intelligent and eager to please.

will walk quietly beside you without pulling as long as you want him to heel. When you stop heeling, indicate to the dog that the exercise is over by verbally praising as you pet him and say 'OK, good dog.' The 'OK' is used as a release word meaning that the exercise is finished and the dog is free to relax.

If you are dealing with a dog who insists on pulling you around, simply 'put on your brakes' and stand your ground until the dog realises that the two of you are not going anywhere until he is beside you and moving at your pace, not his. It may take some time just standing there to convince the dog that you are the leader and you will be the one to decide on the direction and speed of your travel.

Each time the dog looks up at you or slows down to give a slack lead between the two of you, quietly praise him and say, 'Good heel. Good dog.' Eventually, the dog will begin to respond and within a few days he will be walking politely beside you without pulling on the

DID YOU KNOW?
Teach your dog to HEEL in an enclosed area. Once you think the dog will obey reliably and you want to attempt advanced obedience exercises such as off-lead heeling, test him in a fenced in area so he cannot run away.

WEANING OFF FOOD IN TRAINING

Food is used in training new behaviours. Once the dog understands what behaviour goes with a specific command, it is time to start weaning him off the food treats. At first, give a treat after each exercise. Then, start to give a treat

lead. At first, the training sessions should be kept short and very positive; soon the dog will be able to walk nicely with you for increasingly longer distances. Remember also to give the dog free time and the opportunity to run and play when you are done with heel practice.

only after every other exercise. Mix up the times when you offer a food reward and the times when you only offer praise so that the dog will never know when he is going to receive both food and praise and when he is going to receive only praise. This is called a variable ratio reward system and it proves successful because there is always the chance that the owner will produce a treat, so the dog never stops trying for that reward. No matter what, ALWAYS give verbal praise.

OBEDIENCE CLASSES

It is a good idea to enrol in an obedience class if one is available in

Cavaliers love to accompany their owners on any number of outings, from dog shows to obedience classes to family picnics.

your area. If yours is a show dog, ringcraft classes would be more appropriate.. Many areas have dog clubs that offer basic obedience training as well as preparatory classes for obedience competition. There are also local dog trainers who offer similar classes.

At obedience trials, dogs can earn titles at various levels of competition. The beginning levels of competition include basic behaviours such as sit, down, heel, etc. The more advanced levels of competition include jumping, retrieving, scent discrimination and signal work. The advanced levels require a dog and owner to put a lot of time and effort into their training and the titles that can be earned at these levels of competition are very prestigious.

OTHER ACTIVITIES FOR LIFE

Whether a dog is trained in the structured environment of a class or alone with his owner at home, there are many activities that can bring fun and rewards to both owner and dog once they have mastered basic control.

Teaching the dog to help out around the home, in the garden or on the farm provides great satisfaction to both dog and owner. In addition, the dog's help makes life a little easier for his owner and raises his stature as a valued companion to his family. It helps give the dog a purpose by occupying his mind and providing an outlet for his energy.

Hiking is an exciting and healthy activity that the dog can be taught without assistance from more than his owner. The exercise of walking and climbing is good for man and dog alike, and the bond that they develop together is priceless.

If you are interested in participating in organised competition with your Cavalier, there are activities other than obedience in which you and your dog can become involved. Agility is a popular and fun sport where dogs run through an obstacle course that includes various jumps, tunnels and other exercises to test the dog's speed and coordination. The owners run through the course beside their dogs to give commands and to guide them through the course. Although competitive, the focus is on fun— it's fun to do, it's fun to watch and it's great exercise.

DID YOU KNOW?

Success that comes by luck is usually short lived. Success that comes by well-thought-out proven methods is often more easily achieved and permanent. This is the Success Method. It is designed to give you, the puppy owner, a simple yet proven way to help your puppy develop clean living habits and a feeling of security in his new environment.

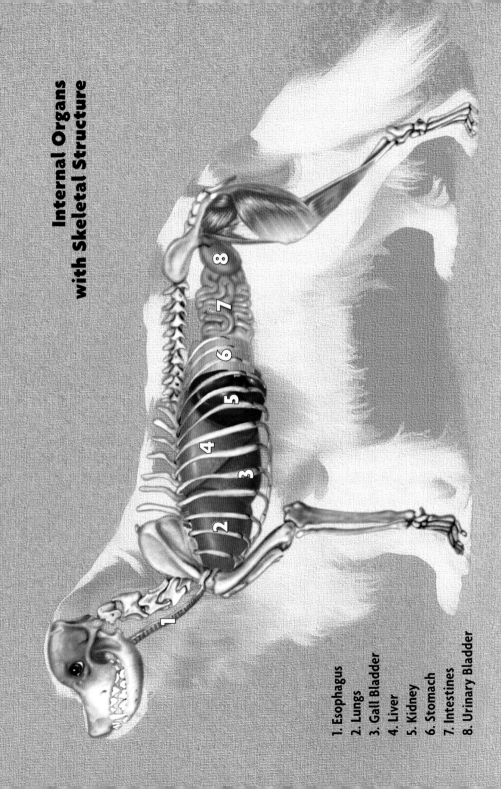

**Internal Organs
with Skeletal Structure**

1. Esophagus
2. Lungs
3. Gall Bladder
4. Liver
5. Kidney
6. Stomach
7. Intestines
8. Urinary Bladder

Dogs suffer many of the same physical illnesses as people. They might even share many of the same psychological problems. Since people usually know more about human diseases than canine maladies, many of the terms used in this chapter will be familiar but not necessarily those used by veterinary surgeons. We will use the term x-ray, instead of the more acceptable term radiograph. We will also use the familiar term symptoms even though dogs don't have symptoms, which are verbal descriptions of the patient's feelings: dogs have clinical signs. Since dogs can't speak, we have to look for clinical signs...but we still use the term symptoms in this book.

As a general rule, medicine is practised. That term is not arbitrary. Medicine is a constantly changing art as we learn more and more about genetics, electronic aids (like CAT scans) and daily laboratory advances. There are many dog maladies, like canine hip dysplasia, which are not universally treated in the same manner. Some veterinary surgeons opt for surgery more often than others do.

SELECTING A VETERINARY SURGEON

Your selection of a veterinary surgeon should not be based upon personality (as most are) but upon

Select a veterinary surgeon convenient to your home. Don't be hesitant to discuss fees, office hours, policies, etc., before deciding on a vet.

their convenience to your home. You want a doctor who is close because you might have emergencies or need to make multiple visits for treatments. You want a doctor who has services that you might require such as a boarding kennel and grooming facilities, as well as pet supplies and a good reputation for ability and responsiveness. There is nothing more frustrating than having to wait a day or more to get a response from your veterinary surgeon.

All veterinary surgeons are

A typical American vet's income categorised according to services performed. This survey dealt with small-animal (pets) practices.

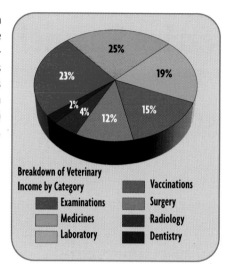

Breakdown of Veterinary Income by Category

- Vaccinations
- Examinations
- Surgery
- Medicines
- Radiology
- Laboratory
- Dentistry

licensed and their diplomas and/or certificates should be displayed in their waiting rooms. There are, however, many veterinary specialties that usually require further studies and internships. There are specialists in heart problems (veterinary cardiologists), skin problems (veterinary dermatologists), teeth and gum problems (veterinary dentists), eye problems (veterinary ophthalmologists), X-rays (veterinary radiologists), and surgeons who have specialities in bones, muscles or other organs. Most veterinary surgeons do routine surgery such as neutering, stitching up wounds and docking tails for those breeds in which such is required for show purposes. When the problem affecting your dog is serious, it is not unusual or impudent to get another medical opinion, although in Britain you

are obliged to advise the vets concerned about this. You might also want to compare costs amongst several veterinary surgeons. Sophisticated health care and veterinary services can be very costly. Don't be bashful about discussing these costs with your veterinary surgeon or his (her) staff. It is not infrequent that important decisions are based upon financial considerations.

PREVENTATIVE MEDICINE
It is much easier, less costly and more effective to practise preventative medicine than to fight bouts of illness and disease. Properly bred puppies come from parents that were selected based upon their genetic disease profile. Their mothers should have been vaccinated, free of all internal and external parasites, and properly nourished. For these reasons, a visit to the veterinary surgeon who cared for the dam (mother) is recommended. The dam can pass on disease resistance to her puppies, which can last for eight

DID YOU KNOW?
You have a valuable dog. If the dog is lost or stolen you would undoubtedly become extremely upset. If you encounter a lost dog, notify the police or the local animal shelter.

First Aid
at a Glance

Burns
Place the affected area under cool water; use ice if only a small area is burnt.

Car accident
Move dog from roadway with blanket; seek veterinary aid.

Bee/Insect bites
Apply ice to relieve swelling; antihistamine dosed properly.

Shock
Calm the dog, keep him warm; seek immediate veterinary help.

Animal bites
Clean any bleeding area; apply pressure until bleeding subsides; go to the vet.

Nosebleed
Apply cold compress to the nose; apply pressure to any visible abrasion.

Spider bites
Use cold compress and a pressurised pack to inhibit venom's spreading.

Bleeding
Apply pressure above the area; treat wound by applying a cotton pack.

Antifreeze poisoning
Immediately induce vomiting by using hydrogen peroxide.

Heat stroke
Submerge dog in cold bath; cool down with fresh air and water; go to the vet.

Fish hooks
Removal best handled by vet; hook must be cut in order to remove.

Frostbite/Hypothermia
Warm the dog with a warm bath, electric blankets or hot water bottles.

Snake bites
Pack ice around bite; contact vet quickly; identify snake for proper antivenin.

Abrasions
Clean the wound and wash out thoroughly with fresh water; apply antiseptic.

Remember: an injured dog may attempt to bite a helping hand from fear and confusion. Always muzzle the dog before trying to offer assistance.

to ten weeks. She can also pass on parasites and many infections. That's why you should visit the veterinary surgeon who cared for the dam.

WEANING TO FIVE MONTHS OLD
Puppies should be weaned by the time they are about two months old. A puppy that remains for at least eight weeks with its mother and litter mates usually adapts better to other dogs and people later in its life.

Some new owners have their puppy examined by a veterinary surgeon immediately, which is a good idea. Vaccination programmes usually begin when the puppy is very young.

The puppy will have its teeth examined and have its skeletal conformation and general health checked prior to certification by the veterinary surgeon. Puppies in certain breeds have problems with their kneecaps, eye cataracts and

other eye problems, heart murmurs and undescended testicles. They may also have personality problems and your veterinary surgeon might have training in temperament evaluation.

VACCINATION SCHEDULING
Most vaccinations are given by injection and should only be done by a veterinary surgeon. Both he and you should keep a record of the date of the injection, the identification of the vaccine and the amount given. Some vets give a first vaccination at eight weeks, but most dog breeders prefer the course not to commence until about ten weeks because of negating any antibodies passed on by the dam. The vaccination scheduling is usually based on a 15-day cycle. You must take your vet's advice as to when to vaccinate as this may differ according to the vaccine used. Most vaccinations immunise your puppy against viruses.

The usual vaccines contain

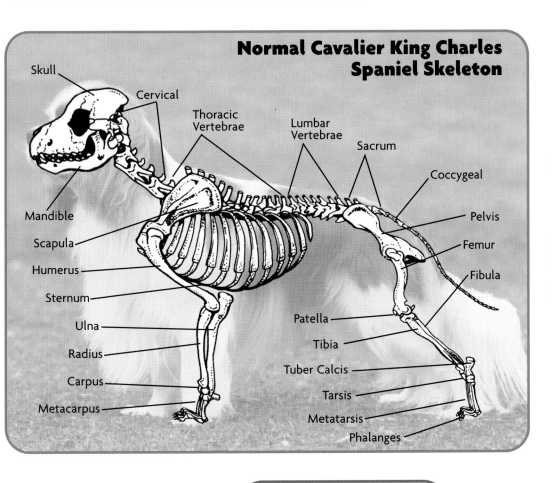

Normal Cavalier King Charles Spaniel Skeleton

Skull
Cervical
Thoracic Vertebrae
Lumbar Vertebrae
Sacrum
Coccygeal
Mandible
Scapula
Humerus
Sternum
Ulna
Radius
Carpus
Metacarpus
Pelvis
Femur
Fibula
Patella
Tibia
Tuber Calcis
Tarsis
Metatarsis
Phalanges

immunising doses of several different viruses such as distemper, parvovirus, parainfluenza and hepatitis. There are other vaccines available when the puppy is at risk. You should rely upon professional advice. This is especially true for the booster-shot programme. Most vaccination programmes require a booster when the puppy is a year old and once a year thereafter. In some

DID YOU KNOW?

Not every dog's ears are the same. Ears that are open to the air are healthier than ears with poor air circulation. Sometimes a dog can have two differently shaped ears. You should not probe inside your dog's ears. Only clean that which is accessible with a wad of soft cotton wool.

HEALTH AND VACCINATION SCHEDULE

AGE IN WEEKS:	3RD	6TH	8TH	10TH	12TH	14TH	16TH	20-24TH
Worm Control	✔	✔	✔	✔	✔	✔	✔	✔
Neutering								✔
Heartworm		✔						✔
Parvovirus		✔		✔		✔		✔
Distemper			✔		✔		✔	
Hepatitis			✔		✔		✔	
Leptospirosis		✔		✔		✔		
Parainfluenza		✔		✔		✔		
Dental Examination			✔					✔
Complete Physical			✔					✔
Temperament Testing			✔					
Coronavirus					✔			
Kennel Cough		✔						
Hip Dysplasia							✔	
Rabies								✔

Vaccinations are not instantly effective. It takes about two weeks for the dog's immune system to develop antibodies. Most vaccinations require annual booster shots. Your veterinary surgeon should guide you in this regard.

cases, circumstances may require more frequent immunisations. Kennel cough, more formally known as tracheobronchitis, is treated with a vaccine that is sprayed into the dog's nostrils. Kennel cough is usually included in routine vaccination, but this is often not so effective as for other major diseases.

DID YOU KNOW?

Vaccines do not work all the time. Sometimes dogs are allergic to them and many times the antibodies, which are supposed to be stimulated by the vaccine, just are not produced. You should keep your dog in the veterinary clinic for an hour after it is vaccinated to be sure there are no allergic reactions.

FIVE MONTHS TO ONE YEAR OF AGE
Unless you intend to breed or show your dog, neutering the puppy at six months of age is recommended. Discuss this with your veterinary surgeon.

By the time your Cavalier King Charles Spaniel is seven or eight months of age, he can be seriously evaluated for his conformation to the standard, thus determining show potential and desirability as a sire or dam. If the puppy is not top class and therefore is not a candidate for a serious breeding programme, most professionals advise neutering the puppy. Neutering has proven to be extremely beneficial to both male and female puppies. Besides eliminating the possibility of pregnancy, it inhibits (but does not prevent) breast cancer in bitches and prostate cancer in male dogs. Under no circumstances should a bitch be spayed prior to her first season.

DOGS OLDER THAN ONE YEAR
Continue to visit the veterinary surgeon at least once a year. There is no such disease as old age, but bodily functions do change with age. The eyes and ears are no longer as efficient. Liver, kidney and intestinal functions often decline. Proper dietary changes, recommended by your veterinary surgeon, can make life more pleasant for the ageing Cavalier King Charles Spaniel and you.

SKIN PROBLEMS IN CAVALIER KING CHARLES SPANIELS
Veterinary surgeons are consulted by dog owners for skin problems more than any other group of diseases or maladies. Dogs' skin is almost as sensitive as human skin and both suffer almost the same ailments. (Though the occurrence

Disease	What is it?	What causes it?	Symptoms
Leptospirosis	Severe disease that affects the internal organs; can be spread to people.	A bacterium, which is often carried by rodents, that enters through mucous membranes and spreads quickly throughout the body.	Range from fever, vomiting and loss of appetite in less severe cases to shock, irreversible kidney damage and possibly death in most severe cases.
Rabies	Potentially deadly virus that infects warm-blooded mammals. Not seen in United Kingdom.	Bite from a carrier of the virus, mainly wild animals.	1st stage: dog exhibits change in behaviour, fear. 2nd stage: dog's behaviour becomes more aggressive. 3rd stage: loss of coordination, trouble with bodily functions.
Parvovirus	Highly contagious virus, potentially deadly.	Ingestion of the virus, which is usually spread through the faeces of infected dogs.	Most common: severe diarrhoea. Also vomiting, fatigue, lack of appetite.
Kennel cough	Contagious respiratory infection.	Combination of types of bacteria and virus. Most common: *Bordetella bronchiseptica* bacteria and parainfluenza virus.	Chronic cough.
Distemper	Disease primarily affecting respiratory and nervous system.	Virus that is related to the human measles virus.	Mild symptoms such as fever, lack of appetite and mucous secretion progress to evidence of brain damage, 'hard pad.'
Hepatitis	Virus primarily affecting the liver.	Canine adenovirus type I (CAV-1). Enters system when dog breathes in particles.	Lesser symptoms include listlessness, diarrhoea, vomiting. More severe symptoms include 'blue-eye' (clumps of virus in eye).
Coronavirus	Virus resulting in digestive problems.	Virus is spread through infected dog's faeces.	Stomach upset evidenced by lack of appetite, vomiting, diarrhoea.

ed at symptoms and not the underlying problem(s). If your dog is suffering from a skin disorder, you should seek professional assistance as quickly as possible. As with all diseases, the earlier a problem is identified and treated, the more successful is the cure.

INHERITED SKIN PROBLEMS

Many skin disorders are inherited and some are fatal. For example, Acrodermatitis is an inherited disease that is transmitted by both parents. The parents, who appear (phenotypically) normal, have a recessive gene for acrodermatitis, meaning that they carry, but are not affected by the disease.

Acrodermatitis is just one example of how difficult it is to prevent congenital dog diseases. The cost and skills required to ascertain whether two dogs should be mated are too high even though puppies with acrodermati-tis rarely reach two years of age.

Other inherited skin problems are usually not as fatal as acroder-matitis. All inherited diseases must be diagnosed and treated by a veterinary specialist. There are active programmes being undertaken by many veterinary pharmaceutical manufacturers to solve most, if not all, of the common skin problems of dogs.

PARASITE BITES

Many of us are allergic to insect bites. The bites itch, erupt and may

of acne in dogs is rare!) For this reason, veterinary dermatology has developed into a speciality practised by many veterinary surgeons.

Since many skin problems have visual symptoms that are almost identical, it requires the skill of an experienced veterinary dermatologist to identify and cure many of the more severe skin disorders. Pet shops sell many treatments for skin problems but most of the treatments are direct-

PET ADVANTAGES

If you do not intend to show or breed your new puppy, your veterinary surgeon will probably recommend that you spay your female or neuter your male. Some people believe neutering leads to weight gain, but if you feed and exercise your dog properly, this is easily avoided. Spaying or neutering can actually have many positive outcomes, such as:

• training becomes easier, as the dog focuses less on the urge to mate and more on you!

• females are protected from unplanned pregnancy as well as ovarian and uterine cancers.

• males are guarded from testicular tumours and have a reduced risk of developing prostate cancer.

Talk to your vet regarding the right age to spay/neuter and other aspects of the procedure.

even become infected. Dogs have the same reaction to fleas, ticks and/or mites. When an insect lands on you, you have the chance to whisk it away with your hand. Unfortunately, when our dog is bitten by a flea, tick or mite, it can only scratch it away or bite it. By the time the dog has been bitten, the parasite has done some of its damage. It may also have laid eggs to cause further problems in the near future. The itching from parasite bites is probably due to the saliva injected into the site when the parasite sucks the dog's blood.

AUTO-IMMUNE SKIN CONDITIONS

Auto-immune skin conditions are commonly referred to as being allergic to yourself, whilst allergies are usually inflammatory reactions to an outside stimulus. Auto-immune diseases cause serious damage to the tissues that are involved.

The best known auto-immune disease is lupus, which affects people as well as dogs. The symptoms are variable and may affect the kidneys, bones, blood chemistry and skin. It can be fatal to both dogs and humans, though it is not thought to be transmissible.

DID YOU KNOW?

Feeding your dog properly is very important. An incorrect diet could affect the dog's health, behaviour and nervous system, possibly making a normal dog into an aggressive one.

It is usually successfully treated with cortisone, prednisone or similar corticosteroid, but extensive use of these drugs can have harmful side effects.

AIRBORNE ALLERGIES

Another interesting allergy is pollen allergy. Humans have hay fever, rose fever and other fevers with which they suffer during the pollinating season. Many dogs suffer the same allergies. When the pollen count is high, your dog might suffer but don't expect them to sneeze and have runny noses like humans. Dogs react to pollen allergies the same way they

Vaccines cannot protect your Cav from everything he will encounter in the great outdoors. While they will protect him from infectious diseases and parasites, you may still have to contend with allergies and skin problems.

react to fleas—they scratch and bite themselves.

Dogs, like humans, can be tested for allergens. Discuss the testing with your veterinary dermatologist.

FOOD PROBLEMS

FOOD ALLERGIES

Dogs are allergic to many foods that are best-sellers and highly recommended by breeders and veterinary surgeons. Changing the brand of food that you buy may not eliminate the problem if the element to which the dog is allergic is contained in the new brand.

Recognising a food allergy is difficult. Humans vomit or have rashes when they eat a food to which they are allergic. Dogs neither vomit nor (usually) develop a rash. They react in the same manner as they do to an airborne or flea allergy: they itch, scratch and bite. Thus making the diagnosis extremely difficult. Whilst pollen allergies and parasite bites are usually seasonal, food allergies are year-round problems.

FOOD INTOLERANCE

Food intolerance is the inability of the dog to completely digest certain foods. Puppies that may have done very well on their mother's milk may not do well on cow's milk. The rest of this food intolerance may be lose bowels, passing gas and stomach pains. These are the only obvious symptoms of food intolerance and that makes diagnosis difficult.

TREATING FOOD PROBLEMS

It is possible to handle food allergies and food intolerance yourself. Put your dog on a diet that it has never had. Obviously if it has never eaten this new food it can't have been allergic or intolerant of it. Start with a single main ingredient in this diet and eliminate the main ingredient by buying a different food that does not have that ingredient. Keep experimenting until the symptoms disappear after one month on the new diet.

ingredient that is not in the dog's diet at the present time. Ingredients like chopped beef or fish are common in dog's diets, so try something more exotic like rabbit, pheasant or even just vegetables. Keep the dog on this diet (with no additives) for a month. If the symptoms of food allergy or intolerance disappear, chances are your dog has a food allergy.

Don't think that the single ingredient cured the problem. You still must find a suitable diet and ascertain which ingredient in the old diet was objectionable. This is most easily done by adding ingredients to the new diet one at a time. Let the dog stay on the modified diet for a month before you add another ingredient. Eventually, you will determine the ingredient that caused the adverse reaction.

An alternative method is to carefully study the ingredients in the diet to which your dog is allergic or intolerable. Identify the

Puppies and adult Cavaliers love the flower garden. Many eat flowers and plants. The pollen and the flowers may cause an allergic reaction. If your dog has an allergy of any kind, as indicated by constant scratching, keep him away from flowers.

A scanning electron micrograph (S. E. M.) of a dog flea, *Ctenocephalides canis*.

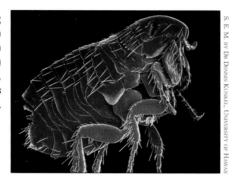

S. E. M. BY DR DENNIS KUNKEL, UNIVERSITY OF HAWAII

(Facing Page) A scanning electron micrograph of a dog or cat flea, *Ctenocephalides*, magnified more than 100x. This has been colourised for effect.

EXTERNAL PARASITES

Of all the problems to which dogs are prone, none is more well known and frustrating than fleas. Fleas, as well as ticks and mites, are difficult to prevent but relatively simple to cure. Parasites that are

harboured inside the body are more difficult to cure but they are easier to control.

FLEAS

To control a flea infestation you have to understand the life cycle of a typical flea. Fleas are basically a summertime problem and their effective treatment (destruction) is environmental. There is no single flea-control medicine (insecticide) that can be used in every flea-infested area. To understand flea control you must apply suitable treatment to the weak link in the life cycle of the flea.

THE LIFE CYCLE OF A FLEA

Fleas are found in four forms: eggs, larvae, pupae and adults. You really need a low-power microscope or hand lens to identify a living flea's eggs, pupae or larva. They spend

Magnified head of a dog flea, *Ctenocephalides canis*.

DID YOU KNOW?

Fleas have been around for millions of years and have adapted to changing host animals.

They are able to go through a complete life cycle in less than one month or they can extend their lives to almost two years by remaining as pupae or cocoons. They do not need blood or any other food for up to 20 months.

They have been measured as being able to jump 300,000 times and can jump 150 times their length in any direction including straight up. Those are just a few of the reasons they are so successful in infesting a dog!

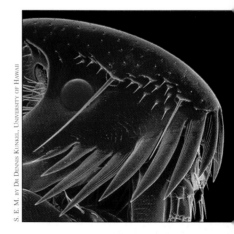

S. E. M. BY DR DENNIS KUNKEL, UNIVERSITY OF HAWAII

The Life Cycle of the Flea

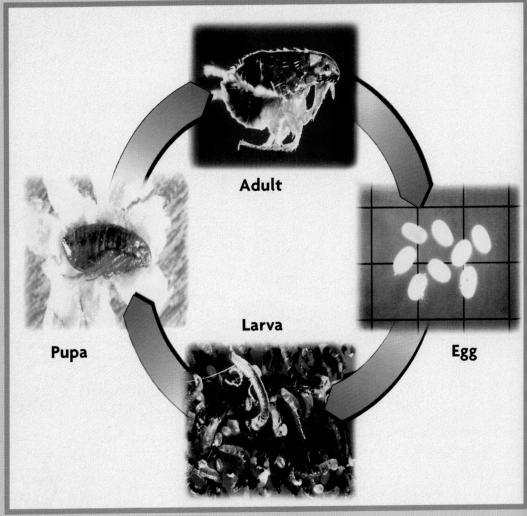

Adult

Pupa

Larva

Egg

The life cycle of the flea was posterised by Fleabusters®. Poster Courtesy of Fleabusters®, R_x for Fleas.

their whole lives on your dog unless they are forcibly removed by brushing, bathing, scratching or biting.

The dog flea is scientifically known as *Ctenocephalides canis* whilst the cat flea is called *Ctenocephalides felis*. Several species infest both dogs and cats.

Fleas lay eggs whilst they are in residence upon your dog. These eggs fall off almost as

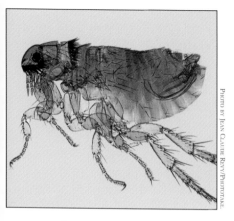

PHOTO BY JEAN CLAUDE REVY/PHOTOTAKE.

soon as they dry (they may be a bit damp when initially laid) and are the reservoir of future flea infestations. If your dog scratches himself and is able to dislodge a few fleas, they simply fall off and await a future chance to attack a dog...or even a person. Yes, fleas from dogs bite people. That's why it is so important to control fleas both on the dog and in the dog's entire environment. You must, therefore, treat the dog and the environment simultaneously.

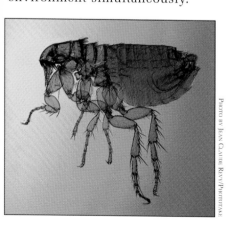

PHOTO BY JEAN CLAUDE REVY/PHOTOTAKE.

DID YOU KNOW?

There are many parasiticides which can be used around your home and garden to control fleas.

Natural pyrethrins can be used inside the house.

Allethrin, bioallethrin, permethrin and resmethrin can also be used inside the house but permethrin has been used successfully outdoors, too.

Carbaryl can be used indoors and outdoors.

Propoxur can be used indoors.

Chlorpyrifos, diazinon and malathion can be used indoors or outdoors and it has an extended residual activity.

A male dog flea, *Ctenocephalides canis.*

The eggs of the dog flea.

Male cat fleas, *Ctenocephalides felis*, are very commonly found on dogs.

115

Dwight R Kuhn's magnificent action photo showing a flea jumping from a dog's back.

PHOTO BY DWIGHT R KUHN

dogs (like window sills, table tops, etc.), so you have to clean all of these areas. The hard floor surfaces (tiles, wood, stone and linoleum) must be mopped several times a day. Drops of food onto the floor are actually food for flea larvae! All rugs and furniture must be vacuumed several times a day. Don't forget closets, under furniture and cushions. A study has reported that a vacuum cleaner with a beater bar can remove only

De-Fleaing the Home

Cleanliness is the simple rule. If you have a cat living with your dog, the matter is more complicated since most dog fleas are actually cat fleas. Cats climb onto many areas that are never accessible to

Human lice look like dog lice; the two are closely related.

PHOTO BY DWIGHT R KUHN

DID YOU KNOW?

Ivermectin is quickly becoming the drug of choice for treating many parasitic skin diseases in dogs.

For some unknown reason, herding dogs like Collies, Old English Sheepdogs and German Shepherds, etc., are extremely sensitive to ivermectin.

Ivermectin injections have killed some dogs, but dogs heavily infected with skin disorders may be treated anyway.

The ivermectin reaction is a toxicosis that causes tremors, loss of power to move their muscles, prolonged dilatation of the pupil of the eye, coma (unconsciousness), or cessation of breathing (death).

The toxicosis usually starts from 4-6 hours after ingestion (not injection), but can begin as late as 12 hours. The longer it takes to set in, the milder is the reaction.

Ivermectin should only be prescribed and administered by a vet.

Some ivermectin treatments require two doses.

20 percent of the larvae and 50 percent of the eggs. The vacuum bags should be discarded into a sealed plastic bag or burned. The vacuum machine itself should be cleaned. The outdoor area to which your dog has access must also be treated with an insecticide.

Your vet will be able to recommend a household insecticidal spray, but this must be used with caution and instructions strictly adhered to.

There are many drugs available to kill fleas on the dog itself, such as the miracle drug ivermectin, and it is best to have the de-fleaing and de-worming supervised by your vet. Ivermectin is effective against many external and internal parasites including heartworms, roundworms, tapeworms, flukes, ticks and mites. It has not been approved for use to control these pests, but veterinary surgeons frequently use it anyway. Ivermectin may not be available in all areas.

STERILISING THE ENVIRONMENT
Besides cleaning your home with vacuum cleaners and mops, you have to treat the outdoor range of your dog. When trimming bushes and spreading insecticide, be careful not to poison areas in which fishes or other animals reside. Remember to choose dog-safe insecticides, but to be absolutely sure, keep your dog away from treated areas.

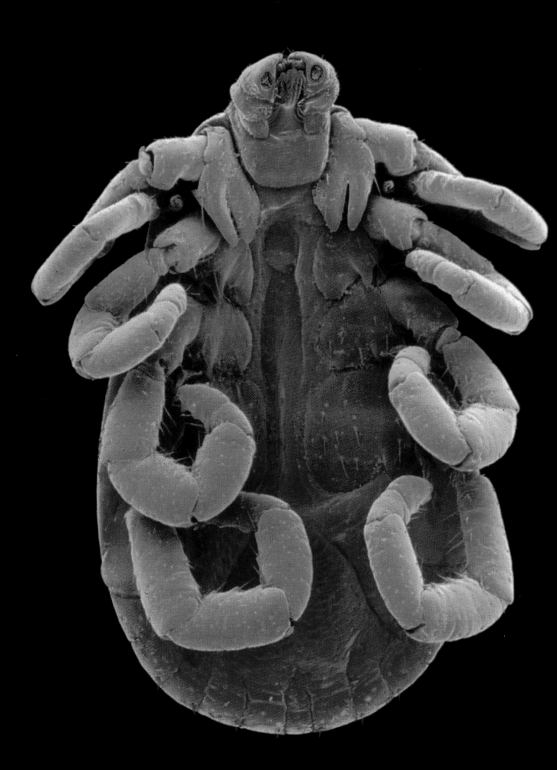

TICKS AND MITES

Though not as common as fleas, ticks and mites are found all over the tropical and temperate world. They don't bite like fleas, they harpoon. They dig their sharp proboscis (nose) into the dog's skin and drink the blood, which is their only food and drink. Dogs can get paralysis, Lyme disease, Rocky Mountain spotted fever (normally found in the U.S.A. only), and many other diseases from ticks and mites. They may live where fleas are found but they also like to hide in cracks or seams in walls wherever dogs live. They are controlled the same way fleas are controlled.

The tick *Dermacentor variabilis* may well be the most common dog tick in many geographical areas, especially where the climate is hot and humid.

Most dog ticks have life expectancies of a week to six months, depending upon climatic conditions. They neither jump nor fly, but crawl slowly and can range up to 5 metres 16 feet) to reach a sleeping or unsuspecting dog.

MANGE

Mange is a skin irritation caused by mites. Some mites are

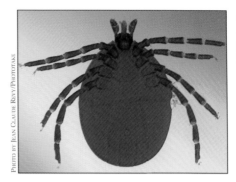

An uncommon dog tick of the genus *Ixode*. Magnified 10x.

PHOTO BY JEAN CLAUDE REVY/PHOTOTAKE.

contagious, like *Cheyletiella*, ear mites, scabies and chiggers. The non-contagious mites are *Demodex*. The most serious of the mites is the one that causes ear-mite infestation. Ear mites are usually controlled with ivermectin.

It is essential that your dog be treated for mange as quickly as possible because some forms of mange are transmissible to people.

(Facing Page) The dog tick, *Dermacentor variabilis*, is probably the most common tick found on dogs. Look at the strength in its eight legs! No wonder it's hard to detach them.

A brown dog tick, *Rhipicephalus sanguineus*, is an uncommon but annoying tick found on dogs.

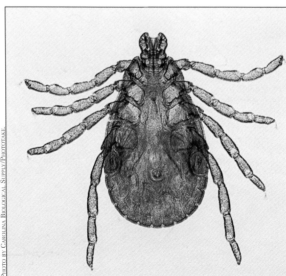

PHOTO BY CAROLINA BIOLOGICAL SUPPLY/PHOTOTAKE.

119

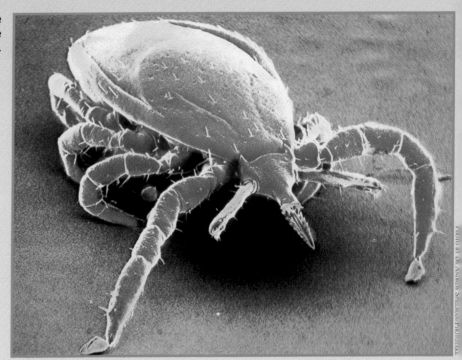

A deer tick, the carrier of Lyme disease.

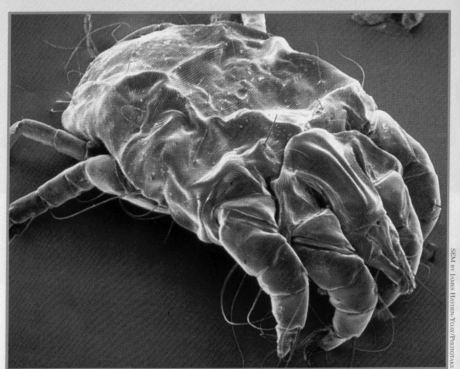

Magnified view of the mange mite, *Psoroptes bovis.*

INTERNAL PARASITES

Most animals—fishes, birds and mammals, including dogs and humans—have worms and other parasites that live inside their bodies. According to Dr Herbert R. Axelrod, the fish pathologist, there are two kinds of parasites: dumb and smart. The smart parasites live in peaceful coopera-tion with their hosts (symbiosis), whilst the dumb parasites kill their host. Most of the worm infections are relatively easy to control. If they are not controlled they eventually weaken the host dog to the point that other medical problems occur, but they are not dumb parasites that direct-ly cause the death of their hosts.

ROUNDWORMS

The roundworms that infect dogs are scientifically known as *Toxocara canis.* They live in the dog's intestine and shed eggs continually. It has been estimated that an average-sized dog produces about 150 grammes of faeces every day. Each gramme of faeces averages 10,000–12,000 eggs of round-worms. All areas in which dogs

DID YOU KNOW?

Ridding your puppy of worms is VERY IMPORTANT because certain worms that puppies carry, such as tapeworms and roundworms, can infect humans.

Breeders initiate a deworming programme at or about four weeks of age. The routine is repeated every two or three weeks until the puppy is three months old. The breeder from whom you obtained your puppy should provide you with the complete details of the deworming programme.

Your veterinary surgeon can prescribe and monitor the programme of deworming for you. The usual programme is treating the puppy every 15 to 20 days until the puppy is positively worm free.

It is not advised that you treat your puppy with drugs that are not recommended professionally.

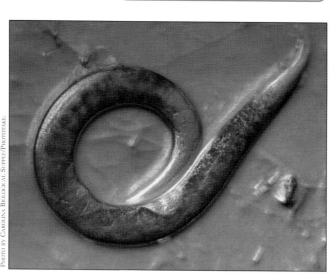

The roundworm can infect both dogs and humans.

The
roundworm
Rhabditis.

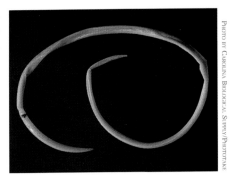

Male and female hookworms, *Ancylostoma caninum*, are uncommonly found in pet or show dogs in Britain. Hookworms may infect other dogs that have exposure to grasslands.

roam contain astronomical numbers of roundworm eggs. The greatest danger of roundworms is that they infect people, too! It is wise to have your dog tested regularly for roundworms.

Pigs also have roundworm infections that can be passed to human and dogs. The typical pig roundworm parasite is called *Ascaris lumbricoides.*

HOOKWORMS

The worm *Ancylostoma caninum* is commonly called the dog hookworm. It is also dangerous to humans and cats. It attaches

itself to the dog's intestines by its teeth. It changes the site of its attachment about six times a day, and the dog loses blood from each detachment. This blood loss can cause iron-deficiency anaemia. Hookworms are easily purged from the dog with many medications, the best of which seems to be ivermectin even though it has not been approved for such use.

In Britain the 'temperate climate' hookworm (*Uncinaria stenocephala*) is rarely found in pet or show dogs, but can occur in hunting packs, racing Greyhounds and sheepdogs because these hookworms can be prevalent wherever dogs are exercised regularly on grassland.

DID YOU KNOW?

Caring for the puppy starts before the puppy is born by keeping the dam healthy and well-nourished. Most puppies have worms, even if they are not evident, so a worming programme is essential. The worms continually shed eggs except during their dormant stage, when they just rest in the tissues of the puppy. During this stage they are not evident during a routine examination.

Average size dogs can pass 1,360,000 roundworm eggs every day.

For example, if there were only 1 million dogs in the world, the world would be saturated with 1,300 metric tonnes of dog faeces. These faeces would contain 15,000,000,000 roundworm eggs.

7 to 31 percent of home gardens and children's play boxes in the U. S. contained roundworm eggs.

Flushing dog's faeces down the toilet is not a safe practice because the usual sewage treatments do not destroy roundworm eggs.

Infected puppies start shedding roundworm eggs at 3 weeks of age. They can be infected by their mother's milk.

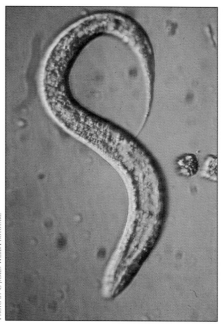

The infective stage of the hookworm larva.

PHOTO BY C JAMES WEBB/PHOTOTAKE

TAPEWORMS

There are many species of tapeworms, many of which are carried by fleas! The dog eats the flea and starts the tapeworm cycle. Humans can also be infected with tapeworms, so don't eat fleas! Fleas are so small that your dog could pass them onto your hands, your plate or your food and make it possible for you to ingest a flea which is carrying tapeworm eggs.

Whilst tapeworm infection is not life threatening in dogs (smart parasite!), it can be the cause of a very serious liver disease for humans. About 50 percent of the humans infected

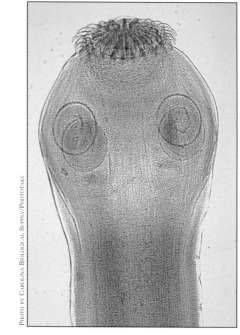

The head and rostellum (the round prominence on the scolex) of a tapeworm, which infects dogs and humans.

PHOTO BY CAROLINA BIOLOGICAL SUPPLY/PHOTOTAKE

with *Echinococcus multilocularis,* causing alveolar hydatis, perish.

HEARTWORMS

Heartworms are thin, extended worms up to 30 cms (12 ins) long that live in a dog's heart and the major blood vessels around it. Your pet may have up to 200 of these worms. The symptoms may be loss of energy, loss of appetite, coughing, the development of a pot belly and anaemia.

Heartworms are transmitted by mosquitoes. The mosquito drinks the blood of an infected dog and takes in larvae with the blood. The larvae, called microfilaria, develop within the body of the mosquito and are passed on to the next dog bitten after the larvae mature. It takes two to three weeks for the larvae to develop to the infective stage within the body of the mosquito. Dogs should be treated at about six weeks of age, then every six months.

Blood testing for heartworms is not necessarily indicative of how seriously your dog is infected. This is a dangerous disease. Dogs in the United Kingdom are not affected by heartworm.

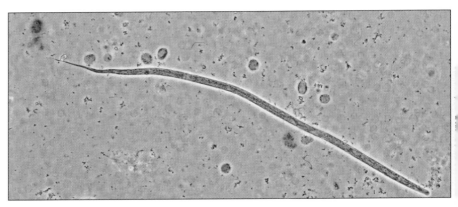

The heartworm, *Dirofilaria immitis.*

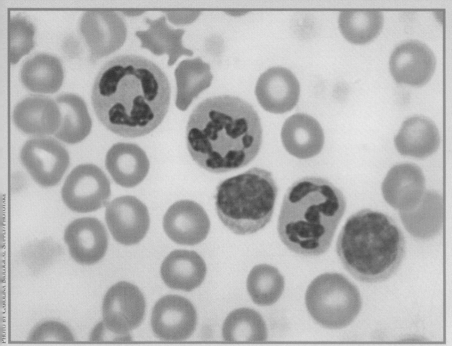

Magnified heartworm larvae, *Dirofilaria immitis.*

The heart of a dog infected with canine heartworm, *Dirofilaria immitis.*

CDS: COGNITIVE DYSFUNCTION SYNDROME
"Old Dog Syndrome"

There are many ways to evaluate old-dog syndrome. Veterinary surgeons have defined CDS (cognitive dysfunction syndrome) as the gradual deterioration of cognitive abilities. These are indicated by changes in the dog's behaviour. When a dog changes its routine response, and maladies have been eliminated as the cause of these behavioural changes, then CDS is the usual diagnosis.

More than half the dogs over 8 years old suffer some form of CDS. The older the dog, the more chance it has of suffering from CDS. In humans, doctors often dismiss the CDS behavioural changes as part of 'winding down.'

There are four major signs of CDS: frequent toilet accidents inside the home, sleeps much more or much less than normal, acts confused, and fails to respond to social stimuli.

SYMPTOMS OF CDS

FREQUENT TOILET ACCIDENTS
- *Urinates in the house.*
- *Defecates in the house.*
- *Doesn't signal that he wants to go out.*

SLEEP PATTERNS
- *Moves much more slowly.*
- *Sleeps more than normal during the day.*
- *Sleeps less during the night.*
- *Walks around listlessly and without a destination goal.*

CONFUSION
- *Goes outside and just stands there.*
- *Appears confused with a faraway look in his eyes.*
- *Hides more often.*
- *Doesn't recognise friends.*
- *Doesn't come when called.*

FAILS TO RESPOND TO SOCIAL STIMULI
- *Comes to people less frequently, whether called or not.*
- *Doesn't tolerate petting for more than a short time.*
- *Doesn't come to the door when you return home from work.*

Cavalier King Charles Spaniel

The term old is a qualitative term. For dogs, as well as their masters, old is relative. Certainly we can all distinguish between a puppy Cavalier King Charles Spaniel and an adult Cavalier King Charles Spaniel—there are the obvious

physical traits, such as size, appearance and facial expressions, and personality traits. Puppies that are nasty are very rare. Puppies and young dogs like to play with children. Children's natural exuberance is a good match for the seemingly endless energy of young dogs. They like to run, jump, chase and retrieve. When dogs grow up and cease their interaction with children, they are often thought of as being

too old to play with the kids.

On the other hand, if a Cavalier King Charles Spaniel is only exposed to people over 60 years of age, its life will normally be less active and it will not seem to be getting old as its activity level slows down.

If people live to be 100 years old, dogs live to be 20 years old. Whilst this is a good rule of thumb, it is very inaccurate. When trying to compare dog years to human years, you cannot make a generalisation about all dogs. You can make the generalisation that 14 years is a good life span for a Cavalier King Charles Spaniel, which is quite good

Your senior Cavalier deserves special attention from his owners. As the dog ages, his world slows down. You owe it to your old chum to be there for him in every way possible.

DID YOU KNOW?
The bottom line is simply that a dog is getting old when YOU think it is getting old because it slows down in its general activities, including walking, running, eating, jumping and retrieving. On the other hand, certain activities increase, like more sleeping, more barking and more repetition of habits like going to the door when you put your coat on without being called.

127

Your veterinary surgeon can evaluate your senior Cavalier and recommend a preventative health care programme suited to your ageing dog.

DID YOU KNOW?

An old dog starts to show one or more of the following symptoms:

• The hair on its face and paws starts to turn grey. The colour breakdown usually starts around the eyes and mouth.

• Sleep patterns are deeper and longer and the old dog is harder to awaken.

• Food intake diminishes.

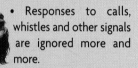

• Responses to calls, whistles and other signals are ignored more and more.

• Eye contacts do not evoke tail wagging (assuming they once did).

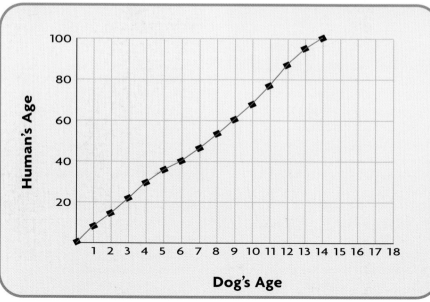

Human's Age (vertical axis: 20, 40, 60, 80, 100)

Dog's Age (horizontal axis: 1 2 3 4 5 6 7 8 9 10 11 12 13 14 15 16 17 18)

compared to, say, a Great Dane. Many large breeds typically live for fewer years than smaller ones. Dogs are generally considered mature within three years, but they can reproduce even earlier. So the first three years of a dog's life are like seven times that of comparable humans. That means a 3-year-old dog is like a 21-year-old human. As the curve of comparison shows, there is no hard and fast rule for comparing dog and human ages. The comparison is made even more difficult, for not all humans age at the same rate...and human females live longer than human males.

WHAT TO LOOK FOR IN SENIORS

Most veterinary surgeons and behaviourists use the seventh year mark as the time to consider a dog a 'senior.' The term 'senior' does not imply that the dog is geriatric and has begun to fail in mind and body. Ageing is essentially a slowing process. Humans readily admit that they feel a difference in their activity level from age 20 to 30, and then from 30 to 40, etc. By treating the seven-year-old dog as a senior, owners are able to implement certain therapeutic and preventive medical strategies with the help of their veterinary surgeons. A senior-care programme should include at least two veterinary visits per year, screening sessions to determine the dog's health status, as well as nutritional counselling. Veterinary surgeons determine the senior dog's health status through a blood smear for a complete blood count, serum chemistry profile with electrolytes, urinalysis, blood pressure check, electrocardiogram, ocular tonometry (pressure on the eyeball) and dental prophylaxis.

Such an extensive

Like humans, dogs age at different rates. It is entirely possible for your Cavalier not to show signs of ageing until he is ten or more. Nonetheless, be wary of his changing needs and behaviour.

programme for senior dogs is well advised before owners start to see the obvious physical signs of ageing, such as slower and inhibited movement, greying, increased sleep/nap periods, and disinterest in play and other activity. This preventative programme promises a longer, healthier life for the ageing dog. Amongst the physical problems common in ageing dogs are the loss of sight and hearing, arthritis, kidney and liver failure, diabetes mellitus, heart disease and Cushing's disease (a hormonal disease).

In addition to the physical manifestations discussed, there are some behavioural changes and problems related to ageing dogs. Dogs suffering from hearing or vision loss, dental discomfort or arthritis can become aggressive. Likewise the near-deaf and/or blind dog may be startled more easily and react in an unexpectedly aggressive manner. Seniors suffering from senility can become more impatient and irritable. Housesoiling accidents are associated with loss of mobility, kidney problems, loss of sphincter control as well as plaque accumulation, physiological brain changes, and reactions to medications. Older dogs, just like young puppies, suffer from separation anxiety, which can lead to excessive barking, whining, housesoiling, and destructive behaviour. Seniors may become fearful of everyday sounds, such as vacuum cleaners, heaters, thunder, and passing traffic. Some dogs have difficulty sleeping, due to discomfort, the need for frequent potty visits, and the like. Owners should avoid spoiling the older dog with too many fatty treats. Obesity is a common problem in older dogs and subtracts years from their lifespan. Keep the senior dog as trim as possible since excessive weight puts additional stress on the body's vital organs. Some breeders recommend supplementing the diet with foods high in fibre and lower in calories. Adding fresh vegetables and marrow broth to the senior's diet makes a tasty, low-calorie, low-fat supplement. Vets also offer specialty diets for senior dogs that are worth exploring.

DID YOU KNOW?

The symptoms listed below are symptoms that gradually appear and become more noticeable. They are not life threatening, however, the symptoms below are to be taken very seriously and a discussion with your veterinary surgeon is warranted:

• Your dog cries and whimpers when it moves and stops running completely.

• Convulsions start or become more serious and frequent. The usual convulsion (spasm) is when the dog stiffens and starts to tremble being unable or unwilling to move. The seizure usually lasts for 5 to 30 minutes.

• Your dog drinks more water and urinates more frequently. Wetting and bowel accidents take place indoors without warning.

• Vomiting becomes more and more frequent.

Your dog, as he nears his twilight years, needs his owner's patience and good care more than ever. Never punish an older dog for an accident or abnormal behaviour. For all the years of love, protection and companionship that your dog has provided, he deserves special attention and courtesies. The older dog may need to relieve himself at 3 a.m. because he can no longer hold it for eight hours. Older dogs may not be able to remain crated for more than two or three hours. It may be time to give up a sofa or chair to your old friend. Although he may not seem as enthusiastic about your attention and petting, he does appreciate the considerations you offer as he gets older.

Your Cavalier King Charles Spaniel does not understand why his world is slowing down. Owners must make the transition into the golden years as pleasant and rewarding as possible.

WHAT TO DO
WHEN THE TIME COMES

You are never fully prepared to make a rational decision about putting your dog to sleep. It is very obvious that you love your Cavalier King Charles Spaniel or you would not be reading this book. Putting a loved dog to sleep is extremely difficult. It is a decision that must be made with your veterinary surgeon. You are usually forced to make the

DID YOU KNOW?
Your senior dog may lose interest in eating, not because he's less hungry but because his senses of smell and taste have diminished. The old chow simply does not smell as good as it once did. Additionally, older dogs use less energy and thereby can sustain themselves on less food.

decision when one of the life-threatening symptoms listed above becomes serious enough for you to seek medical (veterinary) help.

If the prognosis of the malady indicates the end is near and your beloved pet will only suffer more and experience no enjoyment for the balance of its life, then euthanasia is the right choice.

WHAT IS EUTHANASIA?

Euthanasia derives from the Greek meaning good death. In other words, it means the planned, painless killing of a dog suffering from a painful, incurable condition, or who is so aged that it cannot walk, see, eat or control its excretory functions.

Euthanasia is usually accomplished by injection with an overdose of an anaesthesia or barbiturate. Aside from the prick of the needle, the experience is usually painless.

131

There are pet cemeteries to be found in most areas of the world.

HOW ABOUT YOU?

The decision to euthanize your dog is never easy. The days during which the dog becomes ill and the end occurs can be unusually stressful for you. If this is your first experience with the death of a loved one, you may need the comfort dictated by your religious beliefs. If you are the head of the family and have children, you should have involved them in the decision of putting your Cavalier King Charles Spaniel to sleep. Usually your dog can be maintained on drugs for a few days in order to give you ample time to make a decision. During this time, talking with members of your family or even people who have lived through this same experience can ease the burden of your inevitable decision.

THE FINAL RESTING PLACE

Dogs can have some of the same privileges as humans. They can occasionally be buried in their entirety in a pet cemetery which is generally expensive, or if they have died at home can be buried in your garden in a place suitably marked with some stone or newly planted tree or bush. Alternatively they can be cremated and the ashes returned to you, or some people prefer to leave their dogs at the surgery for the vet to dispose of.

All of these options should be discussed frankly and openly with your veterinary surgeon. Do not be afraid to ask financial questions. Cremations can be individual, but a less expensive option is mass cremation, although of course the ashes can not then be returned. Vets can usually arrange cremation services on your behalf, but you must be aware that in Britain if your dog has died at the surgery the vet cannot legally allow you to take your dog's body home.

GETTING ANOTHER DOG?

The grief of losing your beloved dog will be as lasting as the grief of losing a human friend or relative. You cannot go out and buy another grandfather, but you can go out and buy another Cavalier King Charles Spaniel. In most cases, if your dog died of old age (if there is such a thing), it had slowed down considerably. Do you want a new Cavalier King Charles Spaniel puppy to replace it? Or are you better off in finding a more mature Cavalier King Charles Spaniel, say two to three years of age, which will usually be housetrained and will have an already developed personality. In this case, you can find out if you like each other after a few hours of being together.

The decision is, of course, your own. Do you want another Cavalier King Charles Spaniel or perhaps a different breed so as to avoid comparison with your beloved friend? Most people usually buy the same breed because they know (and love) the characteristics of that breed. Then, too, they often know people who have the same breed and perhaps

There are places in some pet cemeteries where your dog's ashes can be kept.

they are lucky enough that one of their friends expects a litter soon. What could be better?

133

Cavalier King Charles Spaniel

When you purchased your Cavalier King Charles Spaniel you should have made it clear to the breeder whether you wanted one just as a loveable companion and pet, or if you hoped to be buying a Cavalier King Charles Spaniel with show prospects. No reputable breeder would sell you a young puppy saying that it was definitely of show quality for so much can go wrong during the early weeks and months of a puppy's development. If you plan to show, what you will hopefully have acquired is a puppy with 'show potential'.

Medals are issued at many prestigious dog competitions.

To the novice, exhibiting a Cavalier King Charles Spaniel in the show ring may look easy but it usually takes a lot of hard work and devotion to do top winning at a show such as the prestigious Crufts, not to mention a little luck too!

The first concept that the canine novice learns when watching a dog show is that each breed first competes against members of its own breed. Once the judge has selected the best member of each breed, provided that the show is judged on a Group system, that chosen dog will compete with other dogs in its group. Finally the best of each group will compete for Best in Show and Reserve Best in Show.

The second concept that you must understand is that the dogs are not actually competing against one another. The judge

DID YOU KNOW?

The Kennel Club divides its dogs into seven Groups: Gundogs, Utility, Working, Toy, Terrier, Hounds and Pastoral.*

*The Pastoral Group, established in 1999, includes those sheepdog breeds previously categorised in the Working Group.

compares each dog against the breed standard, which is a written description of the ideal specimen of the breed. Whilst some early breed standards were indeed based on specific dogs that were famous or popular, many dedicated enthusiasts say that a perfect specimen, described in the standard, has never been bred. Thus the 'perfect' dog never walked into a show ring, has never been bred and, to the woe of dog breeders around the globe, does not exist. Breeders attempt to get as close to this ideal as possible, with every litter, but theoretically the 'perfect' dog is so elusive that it is impossible. (And if the 'perfect' dog were born, breeders and judges would never agree that it was indeed 'perfect.')

WINNING THE TICKET

Earning a championship at Kennel Club shows is the most difficult in the world. Compared to the United States and Canada where it is relatively not 'challenging,' collecting three green tickets not only requires much time and effort, it can be very expensive! Challenge Certificates, as the tickets are properly known, are the building blocks of champions—good breeding, good handling, good training and good luck!

If you are interested in exploring dog shows, your best bet is to join your local breed club. These clubs often host both Championship and Open shows, and sometimes Match meetings and Special Events, all of which could be of interest, even if you are only an onlooker. Clubs also send out newsletters and some organise training days and seminars in order that people may learn more about their chosen breed. To locate the nearest breed club for you, contact The Kennel Club, the ruling body for the British dog world. The Kennel Club governs not only conformation shows but also working trials, obedience trials, agility trials and field trials. The Kennel Club furnishes the rules and regula-

The Cavalier King Charles Spaniel makes a brilliant show dog. If you have acquired a puppy with the intentions of showing, you will need to become acquainted with the procedures of The Kennel Club.

Dog show folk are quite innovative at protecting their Cavalier's coats from the elements. Often vendors sell unique products at the show site, like this doggie coat.

judges to earn the prefix of 'Sh Ch.' or 'Ch.' Note that some breeds must also qualify in a field trial in order to gain the title of full champion. Challenge Certificates are awarded to a very small percentage of the dogs competing, especially as dogs which are already Champions compete with others for these coveted CCs. The number of Challenge Certificates awarded in any one year is based upon the total number of dogs in each breed entered for competition. There three types of Championship Shows, an all-

tions for all these events plus general dog registration and other basic requirements of dog ownership. Its annual show called the Crufts Dogs Show, held in Birmingham, is the largest bench show in England. Every year around 20,000 of the U.K.'s best dogs qualify to partic-ipate in this marvellous show which lasts four days.

The Kennel Club governs many different kinds of shows in Great Britain, Australia, South Africa and beyond. At the most competitive and prestigious of these shows, the Championship Shows, a dog can earn Challenge Certificates, and thereby become a Show Champion or a Champion. A dog must earn three Challenge Certificates under three different

DID YOU KNOW?
Just like with anything else, there is a certain etiquette to the show ring that can only be learned through experience. Showing your dog can be quite intimidating to you as a novice when it seems as if everyone else knows what he's doing. You can familiarise yourself with ring procedure beforehand by taking a class to prepare you and your dog for conformation showing or by talking with an experienced handler. When you are in the ring, listen and pay attention to the judge and follow his/her directions. Remember, even the most skilled handlers had to start somewhere. Keep it up and you too will become a proficient handler before too long!

breed General Championship show for all Kennel Club recognised, a Group Championship Show, limited to breeds within one of the groups, and a Breed Show, usually confined to a single breed. The Kennel Club determines which breeds at which Championship Shows will have the opportunity to earn Challenge Certificates (or tickets). Serious exhibitors often will opt not to participate if the tickets are withheld at a particular show. This policy makes earning championships ever more difficult to accomplish.

Open Shows are generally less competitive and are frequently used as 'practice shows' for young dogs. There are hundreds of Open Shows each year that can be invitingly social events and are great first show experiences for the novice. Even if you're considering just watching a show to wet your paws, an Open Show is a great choice.

Whilst Championship and Open Shows are most important for the beginner to understand, there are other types of shows in which the interested dog owner can participate. Training clubs sponsor Matches that can be entered on the day of the show for a nominal fee. In these introductory-level exhibitions, two dogs are pulled out of a hat and 'matched,' the winner of that match goes on to the next round, and eventually

---

CLASSES AT DOG SHOWS

There can be as many as 18 classes per sex for your breed. Check the show schedule carefully to make sure that you have entered your dog in the appropriate class. Among the classes offered can be: Beginners; Minor Puppy (ages 6 to 9 months); Puppy (ages 6 to 12 months); Junior (ages 6 to 18 months); Beginners (handler or dog never won first place) as well as the following, each of which is defined in the schedule: Maiden; Novice; Tyro; Debutant; Undergraduate; Graduate; Postgraduate; Minor Limit; Mid Limit; Limit; Open; Veteran; Stud Dog; Brood Bitch; Progeny; Brace and Team.

---

only one dog is left undefeated.

Exemption Shows are much more light-hearted affairs with usually only four pedigree classes and several 'fun' classes, all of which can be entered on the day. The proceeds of an Exemption Show must be given to a charity and are sometimes held in conjunction with small agricultural shows. Limited Shows are also available in small number, but entry is restricted to members of the club which hosts the show, although one can usually join the club when making an entry.

Before you actually step into the ring, you would be well

There are many levels and types of dog shows and competitions in which you can enter your Cavalier. Your breeder should be able to help introduce you to the joys of dog showing.

advised to sit back and observe the judge's ring procedure. If it is your first time in the ring, do not be over-anxious and run to the front of the line. It is much better to stand back and study how the exhibitor in front of you is performing. The judge asks each handler to 'stand' the dog, hopefully showing the dog off to his best advantage. The judge will observe the dog from a distance and from different angles, approach the dog, check his teeth, overall structure, alertness and muscle tone, as well as consider how well the dog 'conforms' to the standard. Most importantly, the judge will have the exhibitor move the dog around the ring in some pattern that he or she should specify (another advantage to not going first, but always listen since some judges change their directions, and the judge is always right!) Finally the judge will give the dog one last look before moving on to the next exhibitor.

If you are not in the top three at your first show, do not be discouraged. Be patient and consistent and you may eventually find yourself in the winning lineup. Remember that the winners were once in your shoes and have devoted many hours and much money to earn the placement. If you find that your dog is losing every time and never getting a nod, it may be time to consider a different dog sport or just enjoy your Cavalier King Charles Spaniel as a pet.

HOW TO ENTER A DOG SHOW

1. Obtain an entry form and show schedule from the Show Secretary.
2. Select the classes that you want to enter and complete the entry form.
3. Transfer your dog into your name at The Kennel Club. (Be sure that this matter is handled before entering.)
4. Find out how far in advance show entries must be made. Oftentimes it's more than a couple of months.

WORKING TRIALS

Working trials can be entered by any well-trained dog of any breed, not just Gundogs or Working dogs. Many dogs that earn the Kennel Club Good Citizen Dog award choose to participate in a working trial. There are five stakes at both open and championship levels: Companion Dog (CD), Utility Dog (UD), Working Dog (WD), Tracking Dog (TD), and Patrol Dog (PD). As in conformation shows, dogs compete against a standard and if the dog reaches the qualifying mark, it obtains a certificate. Divided into groups, each exercise must be achieved 70 percent in order to qualify. If the dog achieves 80 percent in the open level, it receives a Certificate of Merit (COM), in the championship level, it receives a

The dogs winning at a conformation show represent many years of competent breeding and training. You cannot expect to go home with the ribbons at your first show.

Qualifying Certificate. At the CD stake, dogs must participate in four groups, Control, Stay, Agility and Search (Retrieve and Nosework). At the next three levels, UD, WD and TD, there are only three groups: Control, Agility and Nosework.

Agility consists of three jumps: a vertical scale up a wall of planks; a clear jump over a basic hurdle with a removable top bar; and a long jump across angled planks.

To earn the UD, WD and TD, dogs must track approximately one-half mile for articles laid from one-half hour to three hours ago. Tracks consist of turns and legs, and fresh ground is used for each participant.

The fifth stake, PD, involves teaching manwork, which is not recommended for every breed and of course is not appropriate for any Toy breed.

FIELD TRIALS AND WORKING TESTS

Working tests are frequently used to prepare dogs for field trials, the purpose of which is to heighten the instincts and natural abilities of gundogs. Live game is not used in working tests. Unlike field trials, working tests do not count toward a dog's record at The Kennel Club, though the same judges often oversee working tests. Field trials began in England in 1947

and are only moderately popular amongst dog folk. Whilst breeders of Working and Gundog breeds concern themselves with the field abilities of their dogs, there is considerably less interest in field trials than dog shows. In order for dogs to become full champions, certain breeds must

DID YOU KNOW?

You can get information about dog shows from kennel clubs and breed clubs:

Fédération Cynologique Internationale
14, rue Leopold II, B-6530 Thuin, Belgium
www.fci.be

The Kennel Club
1-5 Clarges St., Piccadilly, London W1Y 8AB, UK
www.the-kennel-club.org.uk

American Kennel Club
5580 Centerview Dr., Raleigh, NC 27606-3390, USA
www.akc.org

Canadian Kennel Club
89 Skyway Ave., Suite 100, Etobicoke, Ontario M9W 6R4 Canada
www.ckc.ca

qualify in the field as well. Upon gaining three CCs in the show ring, the dog is designated a Show Champion (Sh Ch). The title Champion (Ch) requires that the dog gain an award at a field trial, be a 'special qualifier' at a field trial or pass a 'special show dog qualifier' judged by a field trial judge on a shooting day.

AGILITY TRIALS

Agility trials began in the United Kingdom in 1977 and have since spread around the world, especially to the United States, where the sport enjoys strong popularity. The handler directs his dog over an obstacle course that includes jumps (such as those used in the working trials), as well as tyres, the dog walk, weave poles, pipe tunnels, collapsed tunnels, etc. The Kennel Club requires that dogs not be trained for agility until they are 12 months old. This dog sport intends to be great fun for dog and owner and interested owners should join a training club that has obstacles and experienced agility handlers who can introduce you and your dog to the 'ropes' (and tyres, tunnels and so on).

The Cavalier breed is exceptional in many ways. At agility trials, the breed has proven both trainable and athletic. The Cavalier is one of the few Toy breeds that consistently excels in agility trials.

FÉDÉRATION CYNOLOGIQUE INTERNATIONALE

Established in 1911, the Fédération Cynologique Internationale (FCI) represents the 'world kennel club.' This international body brings uniformity to the breeding, judging and showing of purebred dogs. Although the FCI originally included only four European nations: France, Holland, Austria and Belgium (which remains its headquarters), the organisation today embraces nations on six continents and recognises well over 300 breeds of purebred dog. There are three titles attainable through the FCI: the International Champion, which is the most prestigious; the International Beauty Champion, which is based on aptitude certificates in different countries; and the International Trial Champion, which is based on achievement in obedience trials in different countries. Quarantine laws in England and Australia prohibit most of their exhibitors from entering FCI shows. The rest of the Continent does participate in these impressive canine spectacles, the largest of which is the World Dog Show, hosted in a different country each year. FCI sponsors both national and international shows. The hosting country determines the judging system and breed standards are always based on the breed's country of origin.

Cavaliers can be taught many tricks, especially if there's a tasty treat involved. The time you spend in training your Cavalier will be repaid many times over the lifespan of the dog.

Cavalier King Charles Spaniel

As a Cavalier owner, you have selected your dog so that you and your loved ones can have a companion, a footwarmer, a friend and a four-legged family member. You invest time, money and effort to care for and train the family's new charge. Of course, this chosen canine behaves perfectly! Well, perfectly like a dog. When discussing the Cavalier, owners have much to consider. Most behaviourists and trainers regard the Cavalier as a very responsive and smart canine, able to assimilate hundreds of words and dozens of commands. Although not primarily a working or performance dog, the Cavalier is known to excel in both obedience and agility and can be trained to execute many useful tasks.

THINK LIKE A DOG
Dogs do not think like humans, nor do humans think like dogs, though we try. Unfortunately, a dog is incapable of figuring out how humans think, so the responsibility falls on the owner to adopt a proper canine mindset. Dogs cannot rationalise, and dogs exist in the present moment. Many dog owners make the mistake in training of

Cavaliers do best if they have a lot of love and human companionship. If there are children in your household, encourage them to assist in training your Cavalier.

> **DID YOU KNOW?**
> Dogs and humans may be the only animals that smile. Dogs imitate the smile on their owner's face when he greets a friend. The dog only smiles at its human friends. It never smiles at another dog or cat. Usually it rolls up its lips and shows its teeth in a clenched mouth while it rolls over onto its back begging for a soft scratch.

thinking that they can reprimand their dog for something he did a while ago. Basically, you cannot even reprimand a dog for something he did 20 seconds ago! Either catch him in the act or forget it! It is a waste of your and your dog's time—in his mind, you are reprimanding him for whatever he is doing at that moment.

The following behavioural problems represent some which owners most commonly encounter. Every dog is unique and every situation is unique. No author could purport to solve your Cavalier's problem simply by reading a script. Here we outline some basic 'dogspeak' so that owners' chances of solving behavioural problems are increased. Discuss bad habits with your veterinary surgeon and he/she can recommend a behavioural specialist to consult in appropriate cases. Since behavioural abnormalities are the leading reason owners abandon their pets, we hope that you will make a valiant effort to

DID YOU KNOW?
Dog aggression is a serious problem. NEVER give an aggressive dog to someone else. The dog will usually be more aggressive in a new situation where his leadership is unchallenged and unquestioned (in his mind).

solve your Cavalier's problem. Patience and understanding are virtues that dwell in every pet-loving household.

AGGRESSION
Aggression can be a very big problem in small dogs, though not so in the Cavalier—-thankfully. Aggression, when not controlled, always becomes dangerous. An aggressive dog, no matter the size, may lunge at, bite or even attack a person or another dog. Aggressive behaviour is not to be tolerated. It is painful for a family to watch their dog become unpredictable in his behaviour to the point where they are afraid of him. Whilst not all aggressive behaviour is dangerous, growling, baring teeth, etc., can be frightening: It is important to ascertain why the dog is acting in this manner. Aggression is a display of dominance, and the dog should not have the dominant role in its pack, which is, in this case, your family.

It is important not to challenge an aggressive dog as this could

DID YOU KNOW?
Punishment is rarely necessary for a misbehaving dog. Dogs that are habitually bad probably had a poor education and they do not know what is expected of them. They need training. Disciplinary behaviour on your part usually does more harm than good.

144

pinpoint the cause of your dog's aggression and do something about it. An aggressive dog cannot be trusted, and a dog that cannot be trusted is not safe to have as a family pet. If, very unusually, you find that your pet has become untrustworthy and you feel it

Fortunately, the Cavalier breed on a whole is amongst the most amicable of all dogs. Aggression problems have little documentation in the breed.

provoke an attack. Observe your Cavalier's body language. Does he make direct eye contact and stare? Does he try to make himself as large as possible: ears alert, chest out, tail erect? Height and size signify authority in a dog pack—being taller or 'above' another dog literally means that he is 'above' in the social status. These body signals tell you that your Cavalier thinks he is in charge, a problem that needs to be addressed. An aggressive dog is unpredictable: you never know when he is going to strike and what he is going to do. You cannot understand why a dog that is playful and loving one minute is growling and snapping the next.

The best solution is to consult a behavioural specialist, one who has experience with small dogs, if possible. Together, perhaps you can

DID YOU KNOW?

When a dog bites there is always a good reason for it doing so. Many dogs are trained to protect a person, an area or an object. When that person, area or object is violated, the dog will attack. A dog attacks with its mouth. It has no other means of attack. It never uses teeth for defense. It merely runs away or lays down on the ground when it is in an indefensible situation. Fighting dogs (and there are many breeds which fight) are taught to fight, but they also have a natural instinct to fight. This instinct is normally reserved for other dogs, though unfortunate accidents occur when babies crawl towards a fighting dog and the dog mistakes the crawling child as a potential attacker. If a dog is a biter for no reason, if it bites the hand that feeds it or if it snaps at members of your family, see your veterinary surgeon or behaviourist immediately for to learn how to modify the dog's behaviour.

necessary to seek a new home with a more suitable family and environment, explain fully to the new owners all your reasons for rehoming the dog to be fair to all concerned. In the very worst case, you will have to consider euthanasia.

AGGRESSION TOWARD OTHER DOGS
A dog's aggressive behaviour toward another dog sometimes stems from insufficient exposure to other dogs at an early age. If other dogs make your Cavalier nervous and agitated, he will lash out as a defensive mechanism, though this behaviour is thankfully uncommon in the breed. A dog that has not received sufficient exposure to other canines tends to believe that he is the only dog on the planet. The animal becomes so

> **DID YOU KNOW?**
> DANGER! If you and your on-lead dog are approached by a larger, running dog that is not restrained, walk away from the dog as quickly as possible. Don't allow your dog to make eye contact with the other dog. You should not make eye contact either. In dog terms, eye contact indicates a challenge.

> **DID YOU KNOW?**
> Never scream, shout, jump or run about if you want your dog to stay calm. You set the example for your dog's behaviour in most circumstances. Learn from your dog's reaction to your behaviour and act accordingly

dominant that he does not even show signs that he is fearful or threatened. Without growling or any other physical signal as a warning, he will lunge at and bite the other dog. A way to correct this is to let your Cavalier approach another dog when walking on lead. Watch very closely and at the very first sign of aggression, correct your Cavalier and pull him away. Scold him for any sign of discomfort, and then praise him when he ignores or tolerates the other dog. Keep this up until he stops the aggressive behaviour, learns to ignore the other dog or accepts other dogs. Praise him lavishly for his correct behaviour.

DOMINANT AGGRESSION
A social hierarchy is firmly established in a wild dog pack. The dog wants to dominate those under him and please those above him. Dogs know that there must be a leader. If you are not the obvious choice for emperor, the dog will assume the throne! These conflict-

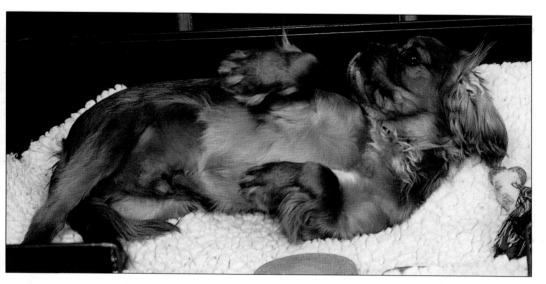

ing innate desires are what a dog owner is up against when he sets about training a dog. In training a dog to obey commands, the owner is reinforcing that he is the top dog in the 'pack' and that the dog should, and should want to, serve his superior. Thus, the owner is suppressing the dog's urge to dominate by modifying his behaviour and making him obedient.

An important part of training is taking every opportunity to reinforce that you are the leader. The simple action of making your Cavalier sit to wait for his food says that you control when he eats and that he is dependent on you for food. Although it may be difficult, do not give in to your dog's wishes every time he whines at you or looks at you with his pleading eyes. It is a constant effort to show the

dog that his place in the pack is at the bottom. This is not meant to sound cruel or inhumane. You love your Cavalier and you should treat him with care and affection. You (hopefully) did not get a dog just so you could boss around another creature. Dog training is not about being cruel or feeling important, it is about moulding the dog's behaviour into what is acceptable

The ultimate sign of surrender is rolling onto its back and exposing its soft belly. This also shows its human friend trust and submission.

DID YOU KNOW?
You should never play tug-of-war games with your puppy. Such games create a struggle for 'top dog' position and teach the puppy that it is okay to challenge you. It will also encourage your puppy's natural tendency to bite down hard and *win*.

and teaching him to live by your rules. In theory, it is quite simple: catch him in appropriate behaviour and reward him for it. Add a dog into the equation and it becomes a bit more trying, but as a rule of thumb, positive reinforcement is what works best.

With a dominant dog, punishment and negative reinforcement can have the opposite effect of what you are after. It can make a dog fearful and/or act out aggressively if he feels he is being challenged. Remember, a dominant dog perceives himself at the top of the social heap and will fight to defend his perceived status. The best way to prevent that is never to give him reason to think that he is in control in the first place. If you are having trouble training your Cavalier and it seems as if he is constantly challenging your authority, seek the help of an obedience trainer or behavioural specialist. A profes-

sional will work with both you and your dog to teach you effective techniques to use at home. Beware of trainers who rely on excessively harsh methods; scolding is necessary now and then, but the focus in your training should always be on positive reinforcement.

If you can isolate what brings out the fear reaction, you can help the dog get over it. Supervise your Cavalier's interactions with people and other dogs, and praise the dog when it goes well. If he starts to act aggressively in a situation, correct him and remove him from the situation. Do not let people approach the dog and start petting him without your express permission. That way, you can have the dog sit to accept petting, and praise him when he behaves properly. You are focusing on praise and on modifying his behaviour by rewarding him when he acts appropriately. By being gentle and by supervising his interactions, you are showing him that there is no need to be afraid or defensive.

SEXUAL BEHAVIOUR

Dogs exhibit certain sexual behaviours that may have influenced your choice of male or female when you first purchased your Cavalier. To a certain extent, spaying/neutering will eliminate these behaviours, but if you are purchasing a dog that you wish to breed, you should be aware of what

DID YOU KNOW?

Your dog inherited the pack-leader mentality. He only knows about pecking order. He instinctively wants to be top dog but you have to convince him that you are boss. There is no such thing as living in a democracy with your dog. You are the dictator, the absolute monarch.

DID YOU KNOW?

Males, whether castrated or not, will mount almost anything: a pillow, your leg or, much to your horror, even your neighbour's leg. As with other types of inappropriate behaviour, the dog must be corrected while in the act, which for once is not difficult. Often he will not let go! While a puppy is experimenting with his very first urges, his owners feel he needs to 'sow his oats' and allow the pup to mount. As the pup grows into a full-size dog, with full-size urges, it becomes a nuisance and an embarrassment. Males always appear as if they are trying to 'save the race,' more determined and stronger than imaginable. While altering the dog at an appropriate age will limit the dog's desire, it usually does not remove it entirely.

you will have to deal with throughout the dog's life.

Female dogs usually have two oestruses per year with each season lasting about three weeks. These are the only times in which a female dog will mate, and she usually will not allow this until the second week of the cycle, but this does vary from bitch to bitch. If not bred during the heat cycle, it is not uncommon for a bitch to experience a false pregnancy, in which her mammary glands swell and she exhibits maternal tendencies toward

toys or other objects.

Owners must further recognise that mounting is not merely a sexual expression but also one of dominance. Be consistent and persistent and you will find that you can 'move mounters.'

CHEWING

The national canine pastime is chewing! Every dog loves to sink his 'canines' into a tasty bone, but sometimes that bone is attached to his owner's hand! Dogs need to chew, to massage their gums, to make their new teeth feel better and to exercise their jaws. This is a natural behaviour deeply imbedded in all things canine. Our role as owners is not to stop the dog's chewing, but to redirect it to chew-worthy objects. Be an informed owner and purchase proper chew toys like strong nylon bones that will not splinter. Be sure that the devices are safe and durable, since your dog's safety is at risk. Again, the owner is responsible for

DID YOU KNOW?

Never allow your puppy to growl at you or bare his tiny teeth. Such behaviour is dominant and aggressive. If not corrected, the dog will repeat the behaviour, which will become more threatening as he grows larger and will eventually lead to biting.

149

ensuring a dog-proof environment. The best answer is prevention: that is, put your shoes, handbags and other tasty objects in their proper places (out of the reach of the growing canine mouth). Direct puppies to their toys whenever you see them tasting the furniture legs or the leg of your trousers. Make a loud noise to attract the pup's attention and immediately escort him to his chew toy and engage him with the toy for at least four minutes, praising and encouraging him all the while.

A Cavalier should know not to jump up on children, though sometimes, in the excitement of saying hello, even a well-trained dog forgets his education.

Some trainers recommend deterrents, such as hot pepper or another bitter spice or a product designed for this purpose, to discourage the dog from chewing unwanted objects. Test out these products yourself before investing in a large quantity.

JUMPING UP
Jumping up is a dog's friendly way of saying hello! Some dog owners do not mind when their dog jumps

up, which is fine for them. The problem arises when guests come to the house and the dog greets them in the same manner—whether they like it or not! However friendly the greeting may be, the chances are

that your visitors will not appreciate your dog's enthusiasm. The dog will not be able to distinguish upon whom he can jump and whom he cannot. Therefore, it is probably best to discourage this behaviour entirely.

Pick a command such as 'Off.' (avoid using 'Down' since you will use that for the dog to lie down) and tell him 'Off' when he jumps up. Place him on the ground on all fours and have him sit, praising him the whole time. Always lavish him with praise and petting when he is

DID YOU KNOW?
Stop a dog from jumping before he jumps. If he is getting ready to jump onto you, simply walk away. If he jumps on you before you can turn away, lift your knee so that it bumps him in the chest. Do not be forceful. Your dog will realise that jumping up is not a productive way of getting attention.

in the sit position. That way you are still giving him a warm affectionate greeting, because you are as excited to see him as he is to see you!

DIGGING

Digging, which is seen as a destructive behaviour to humans, is actually quite a natural behaviour in dogs. Whether or not your dog is one of the 'earth dogs' (also known as terriers), his desire to dig can be irrepressible and most frustrating to his owners. When digging occurs in your garden, it is actually a normal behaviour redirected into something the dog can do in his everyday life. In the wild, a dog would be actively seeking food, making his own shelter, etc. He would be using his paws in a purposeful manner for his survival. Since you provide him with food and shelter, he has no need to use his paws for these purposes, and so the energy that he would be using may manifest itself in the form of little holes all over your garden and flower beds.

Perhaps your dog is digging as a reaction to boredom—it is somewhat similar to someone eating a whole bag of crisps in front of the TV—because they are there and there is not anything better to do! Basically, the answer is to provide the dog with adequate play and exercise so that his mind and paws are occupied, and so that he feels as if he is doing something useful.

Of course, digging is easiest to control if it is stopped as soon as

DID YOU KNOW?
We all love our dogs and our dogs love us. They show their love and affection by licking us. This is not a very sanitary practice as dogs lick and sniff in some unsavory places. Kissing your dog on the mouth is strictly forbidden, as parasites can be transmitted in this manner.

possible, but it is often hard to catch a dog in the act. If your dog is a compulsive digger and is not easily distracted by other activities, you can designate an area on your property where it is okay for him to dig. If you catch him digging in an off-limits area of the garden, immediately bring him to the approved area and praise him for digging there. Keep a close eye on him so that you can catch him in the act—that is the only way to make him understand what is permitted and what is not. If you take him to a hole he dug an hour ago and tell him 'No,' he will understand that you are not fond of holes, or dirt, or flowers. If you catch him whilst he is stifle-deep in your tulips, that is when he will get your message.

BARKING

Dogs cannot talk—oh, what they would say if they could! Instead, barking is a dog's way of 'talking.' It can be somewhat frustrating because it is not always easy to tell what a dog means by his bark—is he excited, happy, frightened or angry? Whatever it is that the dog is trying to say, he should not be punished for barking. It is only when the barking becomes excessive, and when the excessive barking becomes a bad habit, that the behaviour needs to be modified. Fortunately, Cavaliers tend to use their barks more purposefully than most dogs. If an intruder came into your home in the middle of the night and your Cavalier barked a warning, wouldn't you be pleased? You would probably deem your dog a hero, a wonderful guardian and protector of the home. Most dogs are not as discriminate as the Cavalier. For instance, if a friend drops by unexpectedly and rings the doorbell and is greeted with a sudden sharp bark, you would probably be annoyed at the dog. But in reality, isn't this just the same behaviour? The dog does not know any better...unless he sees who is at the door and it is someone he knows, he will bark as a means of vocalising that his (and your) territory is being threatened. Whilst your friend is not posing a threat, it is all the same to the dog. Barking is his means of letting you know that there is an intrusion, whether friend or foe, on your property. This type of barking is instinctive and should not be discouraged.

Excessive habitual barking, however, is a problem that should be corrected early on. As your Cavalier grows up, you will be able to tell when his barking is purposeful and when it is for no reason. You will become able to distinguish your dog's different barks and their meanings. For example, the bark when someone comes to the door will be different from the bark when he is excited to see you. It is similar to a person's tone of voice, except that the dog has to rely totally on tone of voice because he does not have the benefit of using words. An incessant barker will be evident at an early age.

There are some things that encourage a dog to bark. For

DID YOU KNOW?

Barking is your dog's way of protecting you. If he barks at a stranger walking past your house, a moving car or a fleeing cat, he is merely exercising his responsibility to protect his pack (YOU) and territory from a perceived intruder. Since the 'intruder' usually keeps going, the dog thinks his barking chased it away and he feels fulfilled. This behaviour leads your overly vocal friend to believe that he is the 'dog in charge.'

Behaviour

DID YOU KNOW?

To encourage proper barking, you can teach your dog the command 'quiet.' When someone comes to the door and the dog barks a few times, praise him. Talk to him soothingly and when he stops barking, tell him 'quiet' and continue to praise him. In this sense you are letting him bark his warning, which is an instinctive behaviour, and then rewarding him for being quiet after a few barks. You may initially reward him with a treat after he has been quiet for a few minutes.

example, if your dog barks non-stop for a few minutes and you give him a treat to quieten him, he believes that you are rewarding him for barking. He will associate barking with getting a treat, and will keep doing it until he is rewarded.

FOOD STEALING

Is your dog devising ways of stealing food from your coffee table? If so, you must answer the following questions: Is your Cavalier hungry, or is he 'constantly famished' like many dogs seem to be? Face it, some dogs are more food-motivated than others. Some dogs are totally obsessed by the smell of food and can only think of their next meal. Food stealing is terrific fun and always yields a great reward—FOOD, glorious food.

The owner's goal, therefore, is to be sensible about where food is placed in the home, and to reprimand your dog whenever caught in the act of stealing. But remember, only reprimand the dog if you actually see him stealing, not later when the crime is discovered for that will be of no use at all and will only serve to confuse.

BEGGING

Just like food stealing, begging is a favourite pastime of hungry puppies! It yields that same lovely reward—FOOD! Dogs quickly learn that their owners keep the 'good food' for themselves, and that we humans do not dine on dried food alone. Begging is a conditioned response related to a specific stimulus, time and place. The sounds of the kitchen, cans and bottles opening, crinkling bags, the smell of food in preparation, etc., will excite the dog and soon the paws are in the air!

Here is the solution to stopping this behaviour: Never give in to a beggar! You are rewarding the dog for sitting pretty, jumping up, whining and rubbing his nose into you by giving him that glorious reward—food. By ignoring the dog, you will (eventually) force the behaviour into extinction. Note that the behaviour likely gets worse before it disappears, so be sure there are not any 'softies' in the family who will give in to little 'Oliver' every time he whimpers, 'More, please.'

153

SEPARATION ANXIETY

Your Cavalier may howl, whine or otherwise vocalise his displeasure at your leaving the house and his being left alone. This is a normal reaction, no different from the child who cries as his mother leaves him on the first day at school. In fact, constant attention can lead to separation anxiety in the first place. If you are endlessly fussing over your dog, he will come to expect this from you all of the time and it will be more traumatic for him when you are not there. Obviously, you enjoy spending time with your dog, and he thrives on your love and attention. However, it should not become a dependent relationship where he is heartbroken without you.

One thing you can do to minimise separation anxiety is to make your entrances and exits as low-key as possible. Do not give your dog a long drawn-out goodbye, and do not overly lavish him with hugs and kisses when you return. This is giving in to the attention that he craves, and it will only make him miss it more when you are away. Another thing you can try is to give your dog a treat when you leave; this will not only keep him occupied and keep his mind off the fact that you have just left, but it will also help him associate your leaving with a pleasant experience.

You may have to accustom your dog to being left alone in intervals. Of course, when your dog starts whimpering as you

> ### DID YOU KNOW?
>
> There are two drugs specifically designed to treat mental problems in dogs. About 7 million dogs each year are destroyed because owners can no longer tolerate their dogs' behaviour, according to Nicholas Dodman, a specialist in animal behaviour at Tufts University in Massachusetts.
>
> The first drug, Clomicalm, is prescribed for dogs suffering from 'separation anxiety,' which is said to cause them to react when left alone by barking, chewing their owners' belongings, drooling copiously, or defecating or urinating inside the home.
>
> The second drug, Anipryl, is recommended for canine cognitive dysfunction or 'old dog syndrome,' a mental deterioration that comes with age. Such dogs often seem to forget that they were housebroken, where their food bowls are, and they may even fail to recognise their owners.
>
> A tremendous human-animal-bonding relationship is established with all dogs, particularly senior dogs. This precious relationship deteriorates when the dog does not recognise his master. The drug can restore the bond and make senior dogs feel more like their old selves.

approach the door, your first instinct will be to run to him and comfort him, but do not do it! Really—eventually he will adjust and be just fine if you take it in small steps. His anxiety stems from being placed in an unfamiliar situation; by familiarising him with being alone he will learn that he is okay. That is not to say you should purposely leave your dog home alone, but the dog needs to know that, whilst he can depend on you for his care, you do not have to be by his side 24 hours a day.

When the dog is alone in the house, he should be confined to his designated dog-proof area of the house. This should be the area in which he sleeps and already feels comfortable so he will feel more at ease when he is alone.

COPROPHAGIA

Faeces eating is, to most humans, one of the most disgusting behaviours that their dog could engage in, yet to the dog it is perfectly normal. It is hard for us to understand why a dog would want to eat its own faeces. He could be seeking certain nutrients that are missing from his diet; he could be just plain hungry; or he could be attracted by the pleasing (to a dog) scent. Whilst coprophagia most often refers to the dog eating his own faeces, a dog may just as likely eat that of another animal as well if he comes across

it. Vets have found that diets with a low digestibility, containing relatively low levels of fibre and high levels of starch, increase coprophagia. Therefore, high-fibre diets may decrease the likelihood of dogs' eating faeces. Both the consistency of the stool (how firm it feels in the dog's mouth) and the presence of undigested nutrients increase the likelihood. Dogs often find the stool of cats and horses more palatable than that of other dogs. Once the dog develops diarrhoea from faeces eating, it will likely quit this distasteful habit.

To discourage this behaviour, first make sure that the food you are feeding your dog is nutritionally complete and that he is getting enough food. If changes in his diet do not seem to work, and no medical cause can be found, you will have to modify the behaviour before it becomes a habit through environmental control. The best way to prevent your dog from eating his stool is to make it unavailable—clean up after he eliminates and remove any stool from the garden. If it is not there, he cannot eat it.

Reprimanding for stool eating rarely impresses the dog. Vets recommend distracting the dog whilst he is in the act of stool eating. Coprophagia is seen most frequently in pups 6 to 12 months of age, and usually disappears around the dog's first birthday.

INDEX

*Page numbers in **boldface** indicate illustrations.*

Acrodermatitis 108
Adult diets 62
Age 84
Aggression 144
—dominant 146
—toward other dogs 146
Agility trials 99, 140-141
Airlines 73
Alansmere Aquarius 15
Allergies
—airborne 109
—food 110
Amelia of Laguna 15
Anaemia 122, 124
Ancylostoma caninum 122, **122**
Ann's Son 13, 14
Ascaris lumbricoides 122
Australia 17
Axelrod, Herbert R. 121
Barking 152
Bathing 67
Begging 153
Behavioural problems 143
Belinda of Saxham 14
Black and tan 16, 24
Blenheim 16, 23
Boarding 74
Body language 145
Bones 45, 149
Boredom 151
Bowls 46
Breed clubs 36
Breed standard 29-33
Breeder 36
Brown dog tick **119**
Brushing 65
Burial 133
Buying 36
Canada 16
Cars 72
Cat 90
Cat flea 114, **115**
Cavalier King Charles Spaniel
    Club 15
CDS 126
Challenge Certificates 136
Champion 136, 141

Championship shows 136
Charles I 9
Charles II 10
Chew toys 149
Chewing 86, 149
Cheyletiella 119
Choke collars 46
Coat 23, 37
Cognitive dysfunction
    syndrome 126
Collar 46, 90
Colostrum 61
Colours 23
Come 94
Commands 92
Coprophagia 155
Coronavirus 107
Crate 43, 59, 72, 85, 87
Crate training 87
Crufts Dog Show 136
Crying 58
Ctenocephalides **113**
Ctenocephalides canis **112, 114, 115**
—eggs **115**
Ctenocephalides felis 114, **115**
Cumberland, Duke and
    Duchess of 11
Cushing's disease 104
Dash 11
Daywell Roger 15
Defleaing the house 116
Demodex 119
Dermacentor variabilis **118, 119**
Destructive behaviour 130, 149, 151, 153
Development schedule 84
Dew claws 26
Deworming programme 121
Diets
—adults 62
—puppy 60
—seniors 63
Digging 151
Dirofilaria immitis **124-125**
Discipline 89

Distemper 107
Dog flea **112,** 114, **115**
—eggs **115**
Dog lice **116**
Dog tick **119**
Down 93
Drying 68
Ear cleaning 69
Ear mites 70, 119
Echinococcus multilocularis 124
Edward VII 12
Eldridge, Roswell 13, 14
English Toy Spaniel **15,** 16
Euthanasia 131
Exemption shows 137
Exercise 64
External parasites 112
Eye problems 27
Faeces eating 155
Family introduction to pup 52
FCI 16, 142
Fear period 55
Fédération Cynologique
    Internationale 16, 142
Fence 50
Field trials 140
Fleas 112-117
Food 60
Food allergy 110
Food intolerance 110
Food stealing 153
Food treats 98
Gainsborough 9
Germany 16
Good Citizen Dog award 139
Gredin 11
Grooming 24-25
Handling 138
Health considerations 26-27
Heart problems 26
Heartworm **124-125**
Heel 96
Hepatitis 107
Hereditary cataracts 27
Hiking 99
Holland 16
Home preparation 42

Hookworm 122, **122**
—larva 123
House of Orange 10
House of Stuart 9
Housebreaking 81
Housebreaking schedule 86
Identification 75
Intelligence 26
Internal parasites 121
Italy 16
Ivermectin 116-117, 119
Ixode **119**
James II 10
Judge 138
Jumping up 150
Kennel Club 12, 14, 136
—breed standard 29-33
Kennel cough 106-107
King Charles Spaniel 9, 10 **15,**
16
King Charles Spaniel Club 12
Kuhn, Dwight R. 116
Landseer, Edwin 13
Lead 45, 90
Leptospirosis 107
Life cycle of the flea 114
Life expectancy 22, 127
Limited shows 137
Lockwood, Barbara 17
Lupus 109
Lyme disease 119
Mange 119
Mange mite **120**
Marlborough, Duchess of 11
Marlborough, Duke of 10
Mary I 9
Mary Queen of Scots 9
Matches 137
Milk 61
Mite infestation 70
Mites 119, **120**
Moro, Antonio 9
Mosquitoes 124
Mounting 149
Multi-focal retinal
dysplasia 27
Nail clipping 70
Negative reinforcement 148
Neutering 107
New South Wales Club 17

New Zealand 15, 17
Nipping 58
Obedience class 78, 98
Obesity 26, 64, 130
Oestrus 149
Off 150
Old dog syndrome 126
Open shows 137
Owner responsibility 34
Owner suitability 20
Ownership 39
Parasites
—bites 108
—external 112
—internal 121
Parasiticides 115
Pargeter Flashback 17
Parvovirus 107
Pepys, Samuel 10
Personality 20, 26
Philip of Spain 9
Pollen allergy 109
Psoroptes bovis **120**
Pug 10, 12, **12**
Punishment 90, 148
Puppy 34
—food 60
—health 104
—problems 55, 57
—training 79
Puppy-proofing your home
48
Rabies 107
Reynolds 9
Rhabditis **122**
Rhipicephalus sanguineus
119
Rocky Mountain spotted
fever 119
Rogue 10
Roundworm **121-122**
Ruby 16, 24
Sales documentation 38
Seasonal cycles 149
Senior 129
Senior diets 63
Separation anxiety 59, 130,
154
Sexual behaviour 148
Sheldon, Margaret 17

Show champion 136, 141
Sit 92
Size 19
Skin problems 107
—auto-immune 109
—inherited 108
'Snorting' 27
Socialisation 55
Soyland Begonia 17
Standard 29-33, 135
Stay 94
Stealing food 153
Stubbs 9
Sugar Crisp of Ttiweh 15
Sweden 16
Tail docking 25-26
Tapeworms 121, 123
Thorndike, Dr Edward 90
Thorndike's Theory of
Learning 90
Tickets 137
Ticks **118,** 119
Titian 9
Toxocara canis 121
Toy 150
Toy Spaniel Club 12
Toy Spaniel 13
Toys 44, 149
Tracheobronchitis 106
Training 57
Training equipment 90
Travelling 72
Treats 91
Tricolour 16, 23-24
Umbilical hernias 37
Uncinaria stenocephala 122
Vaccinations 37, 104
Van Dyck 9
Veterinary surgeon 51, 101,
104, 117, 121
Victoria 11
Water 63
Water dogs 27
Whining 58
William and Mary 10
Working tests 140
Working trials 139
World Dog Show 16, 142
World War I 12
Worming 37

My Cavalier King Charles Spaniel

PUT YOUR PUPPY'S FIRST PICTURE HERE

Dog's Name _____

Date _____ Photographer _____